Kafka's Soup

A complete history of world literature in 17 recipes

Kafka's Soup

A complete history of world literature
in 17 recipes

Written and illustrated by
Mark Crick

Granta Books
London

Granta Publications, 2/3 Hanover Yard, Noel Road, London N1 8BE

This extended paperback edition first published in Great Britain by
Granta Books, 2007
First published in Great Britain by Libri Publications Ltd, 2005

A CIP catalogue record for this book
is available from the British Library.

1 3 5 7 9 10 8 6 4 2

ISBN 978-1-86207-983-0

Typeset by M Rules

Printed and bound in Malta by Gutenberg Press Limited

Contents

LAMB WITH DILL SAUCE *à la* Raymond Chandler   7

TARRAGON EGGS *à la* Jane Austen   10

QUICK MISO SOUP *à la* Franz Kafka   16

RICH CHOCOLATE CAKE *à la* Irvine Welsh   20

TIRAMISU *à la* Marcel Proust   29

COQ AU VIN *à la* Gabriel Garcia Marquez   36

MUSHROOM RISOTTO *à la* John Steinbeck   44

BONED STUFFED POUSSINS *à la* Marquis de Sade   48

CLAFOUTIS GRANDMÈRE *à la* Virginia Woolf   60

FENKATA *à la* Homer   64

VIETNAMESE CHICKEN *à la* Graham Greene   70

SOLE A LA DIEPPOISE *à la* Jorge Luis Borges   74

CHEESE ON TOAST *à la* Harold Pinter   82

ONION TART *à la* Geoffrey Chaucer   89

RÖSTI *à la* Thomas Mann   93

MOULES MARINIÈRE *à la* Italo Calvino   102

PLUM PUDDING *à la* Charles Dickens   110

Lamb with Dill Sauce
à la Raymond Chandler

1kg lean leg of lamb, cut into large chunks
1 onion, sliced
1 carrot, cut into sticks
1 tablespoon crushed dill seeds, or 3–4 sprigs fresh dill
1 bay leaf
12 peppercorns
1/2 teaspoon salt
850ml chicken stock
50g butter
1 tablespoon plain flour
1 egg yolk
3 tablespoons cream
2 teaspoons lemon juice

I sipped on my whisky sour, ground out my cigarette on the chopping board and watched a bug trying to crawl out of the basin. I needed a table at Maxim's, a hundred bucks and a gorgeous blonde; what I had was a leg of lamb and no clues. I took hold of the joint. It felt cold and damp, like a coroner's handshake. I took out a knife and cut the lamb into pieces. Feeling the blade in my hand I sliced an onion, and before I knew what I was doing a carrot lay in pieces on the slab. None of them moved. I threw the lot into a pan with a bunch of dill stalks, a bay leaf, a handful of peppercorns and a pinch of salt.

They had it coming to them, so I covered them with chicken stock and turned up the heat. I wanted them to boil slowly, just about as slowly as anything can boil. An hour and a half and a half-pint of bourbon later they weren't so tough and neither was I. I separated the meat from the vegetables and covered it to keep it moist. The knife was still in my hand but I couldn't hear any sirens.

In this town the grease always rises to the top, so I strained the juice and skimmed off the fat. I added more water and put it back on the heat. It was time to deal with the butter and flour, so I mixed them together into a paste and added it to the stock. There wasn't a whisk, so using my blackjack I beat out any lumps until the paste was smooth. It started to boil, so I let it simmer for two minutes.

I roughed up the egg yolk and cream and mixed in some of the hot sauce before putting the lot back into the pan. I put the squeeze on a lemon and it soon juiced. It was easy. It was much too easy, but I knew if I let the sauce boil the yolk was gonna scramble.

By now I was ready to pour the sauce over the meat and serve, but I wasn't hungry. The blonde hadn't showed. She was smarter than I thought. I went outside to poison myself, with cigarettes and whisky.

9

Tarragon Eggs

à la Jane Austen

40g butter
4 eggs
Ground pepper
Pinch of salt
2 teaspoons tarragon (fresh or dried)

It is a truth universally acknowledged that eggs, kept for too long, go off. The eggs of Oakley Farm had only recently been settled in the kitchen at Somercote, but already Mrs B—— was planning a meal that would introduce them to the neighbourhood with what she hoped would be universal acceptance. Her eggs had been strongly endowed by nature with a turn for being uniformly agreeable and she hoped to see at least a half-dozen of them make fine matches in the coming week. The arrival of a newcomer in the parish presented the perfect opportunity and Mrs B—— wasted no time in sending out invitations to a luncheon.

Many hours had been spent discussing the merits of one dish over another with her neighbour, Lady Cumberland. The two ladies took prodigious care when considering the advantages of tea over coffee and whether the toast should be white or brown, subjects on which Lady Cumberland delivered her opinions in so decisive a manner that Mrs B—— dared not disagree. Lady Cumberland was no

The Pocket Union of Miss Egg and Monsieur Stragon
after Rowlandson

supporter of the new cooking, which she blamed, first, for bringing ingredients of obscure origin into undue distinction, and secondly, for raising cooks to honours of which their fathers and grandfathers had never dreamt. As a sacrifice to propriety, Mrs B—— agreed that the dish would be a traditional one.

With the day of the luncheon drawing near, Mrs B—— was suffering terribly with her nerves. The event that she had announced with such anticipation had ceased to be a source of pleasure. On the contrary, it was unfair of the local ladies to allow the burden of organising such gatherings to fall so often to her; and was it not strange that Mrs Eliot had not returned the courtesy of the dinner that she had given a fortnight past? Such were the mutterings of Mrs B—— as she paced the garden seeking inspiration, when the sound of a carriage crossing the lawn announced the arrival of Lady Cumberland, who suggested a small rehearsal. So it was that the two neighbours found themselves in the kitchen at Somercote, still busily searching for a proper suitor for the eggs. While Lady Cumberland sat drinking tea, Mrs B—— chose for her employment to search the pantry, stalking the absent suitor.

"Parsley might do," said she. The herb was a regular at the house and the chance that it might combine well with her eggs meant that Mrs B—— could only think well of it:

"Good-looking, with an easy and unaffected manner." Lady Cumberland's reaction was unequivocal: "Too much curl to its leaf, and too often seen in great bunches at fishmongers. It would be a most unhappy connection."

Mrs B—— was not used to disagreeing with the better informed mind of Lady Cumberland, and now, her every cherished opinion of parsley's worth overthrown, she turned her eye to rarer visitors, including the tarragon. She had always thought tarragon a difficult herb and hard to please. "It refuses to grow here, it refuses to grow there, but fancies itself so very great, disappearing every winter I know not where. I quite detest the plant."

"French tarragon is an aristocrat among herbs, and although I think it too good for your eggs, I cannot deny that it would be a fine match for them," said Lady Cumberland. Mrs B—— received the remark with all the forbearance of civility and the slight on her eggs went unremarked. But a recommendation from so high a source as Lady Cumberland could not be ignored, and Mrs B——'s contempt for the noble tarragon was soon forgotten. The possibility that her eggs might find themselves cooked with the aristocratic herb sent Mrs B—— into such a state of excitement that Lady Cumberland would have risen to leave were it not for the promise of luncheon. Instead she instructed her host to produce the dish without delay: "I suggest you begin."

Mrs B—— obliged by beating the eggs slightly to break up yolks and whites. On Lady Cumberland's instruction she then passed the eggs through a sieve to remove the thread and further mix the white and yolk without creating the froth that can be "so unsightly". No sooner had such an end been reached than she added the tarragon, which was by now high in her good graces. She could barely hold back her raptures at how good the tarragon and eggs looked together and anticipated the happy moment when she would see them united, on toast.

Taking half the butter, Mrs B—— spread it around the pan, and pronounced it to be the most tractable of ingredients. The remaining butter she added in small lumps to the mixture, together with salt and pepper, before cooking the whole over a gentle heat, stirring constantly and scraping the bottom of the pan as she did so. As soon as the attachment seemed to strengthen she removed the dish from the heat and kept stirring; the warmth of the pan was sufficient to complete the cooking before the eggs became too dry.

This delightful union Mrs B—— then served with toasted bread, and with so much good taste and true merit that, when Lady Cumberland was obliged to declare the dish acceptable, the happiness of her guests was assured. And so it proved to be the case, with the possible exception of Mrs

Eliot, who, when she detailed the particulars to her husband, remarked on the lack of finery or parade in the table setting and on the inferiority of the dish next to her own eggs benedict. But, in spite of all these deficiencies, the hopes, the sensitivities and the appetites of the small band of true friends who gathered for luncheon were fully answered in the perfect success of the union.

Quick Miso Soup
à la Franz Kafka

3 dessertspoons fermented miso
150g silken tofu
4–5 small mushrooms
A few leaves of dried wakame
Soy sauce

K. recognised that if a man is not always on his guard
this kind of thing can happen. He was looking into the
refrigerator and found it to be almost completely bare, apart
from some mushrooms, which he began to slice. His guests
sat waiting at the table and yet he appeared to have little to
offer them. Whether he had invited them or whether they
had arrived uninvited was not clear. If it were the first case he
was angry with himself for failing to engage a cook for the
evening so that he might command some authority at the
table; for now his visitors were looking towards him as
though he were a subordinate whose inefficiency was
delaying their dinner. But in the second case they could
hardly expect to be fed, arriving unexpectedly at such a time.
The sound of a kettle boiling brought his attention back to
the food and at the same time he noticed a jar of fermented
miso and a block of silken tofu, perhaps left by his landlady.
He placed three spoonfuls of the miso into a saucepan and
poured on two pints of hot water, shielding the process from

Soup

the panel as he did so. He became angry with himself for thinking of the new arrivals as a panel; they had not announced their purpose in calling on him and as yet he did not know what position each of them held. Their manner suggested, perhaps, that they were higher officials but it was also quite possible that he was their superior and they were calling on him merely to create a good impression.

With shame K. realised that he had not offered his guests anything to drink, but when he looked up he saw that a bottle was open on the table and the judges were already enjoying his wine. He found it abominable that they had served themselves without permission, but he knew their impertinence was not without significance. K. decided to shame them for their rudeness. "How is the wine?" he called. But the ruse backfired. "It would be better with some food," they chorused. "But since you have not even granted us the courtesy of dressing for dinner we do not have high hopes." K. could scarcely believe it as he noticed with discomfort that he was, indeed, in shirt and drawers.

When the soup was simmering, K. cut the tofu into one-centimetre cubes and dropped it into the steaming pan with the mushrooms and some wakame. Looking out of the window into the darkness he noticed that a girl was watching from the neighbouring house. The girl's severe expression was not unattractive to K., but the thought that she was deriving some pleasure from his situation sent him into a fury and he struck the worktop with his fist. It occurred to him that she might in some way be attached to the interrogation commission or could influence his case, and he looked beseechingly towards her, but she had backed away now and he might already have thrown away any advantages that his situation bestowed upon him. In two minutes the soup was ready. K. poured it into bowls and served his visitors. One of the four chairs around the table had been removed and, not without discomfort, K. saw that the panel was making no effort to make room for him. He added a splash of soy sauce to each of the bowls while the elder of the three judges addressed the others as if K. were invisible. "He needs to rid himself of a great many illusions; it's possible he imagines that we are subordinates calling on him to win his approval."

K.'s feeling that he was an outsider at his own dinner party was not unfamiliar. He was sorry that he was not dressed in his grey suit: its elegant cut had caused a sensation among his friends, and it was of the utmost importance to create a good impression in these situations. It was essential for a man in his position not to appear surprised by events and, as the interrogation commission divided the contents of K's bowl between them, K. stood still and tried to collect himself, for he knew that great demands would be made upon him and the soup might yet influence the outcome of his case.

Rich Chocolate Cake
à la Irvine Welsh

250g butter
500g sugar
40g cocoa
250ml coffee
150g milk chocolate
2 eggs
275g self-raising flour
375ml port

For the icing:
200g dark chocolate
100g caster sugar
100ml double cream
100ml Kahlúa (optional)

Ah make ma way back to the shithole that ah call home, wi aw the gear ah need, but ah kin barely move. Ma heid is throbbing like it's aboot tae burst, showering passers-by wi brain and bone, and ah'm so fuckin frail ma legs could snap as ah climb the stairs. Ah hope nae fucker's seen me coming back. Ah dinnae want to share any of this shite wi ma so-called friends.

Ah drop a packet of butter intae the pan and light the flame beneath it. As it melts, ah pour on the sugar, watching

IGGY POP

Plate 6.

After Hogarth

A Quality Fuckin Cook-Up

Rich Chocolate Cake

the white grains dissolve intae the golden brown liquid. They're dissolving cleanly; it's good fuckin shite. Ma hands are shaking as ah sprinkle the brown powder of the cocoa intae the pan and when ah drop in the bar of chocolate ah have the satisfaction of watching it melt straight away. This is a quality fuckin cook-up.

As the mixture begins to bubble and spit ah find ah'm oot of coffee, but a quick scramble under the settee produces a mug of the stuff and ah'm no fuckin goin back doon those stairs. Intae the brew it goes. The pain in ma heid is beginning to subside and, what wi the smell of the gear cookin and the calming sight of the gas flame, ah'm feeling better already.

Ah take the pan off the heat while ah crack two eggs into a jug. Ma eyes focus long enough oan the shells tae read the crack-by date: the bastards want me tae throw them oot and buy more. Mebbe the hen that laid them is sitting in the freezer doon at Scotmid, but ah know they keep for months. There's nae need tae beat the eggs: the 14.22 from King's Cross goes by the windae and stirs every fuckin thing, including me. Ah measure oot the flour and at the sight of such a mountain of white powder ah'm tempted tae stick ma nose in. Ah add the eggs and flour to the mixture and pour oan a drop of port. Ah hae a drop masel; it's no bad, so ah put some more intae the pan. The bottle's soon finished.

Ah've drunk half and the other half's goan intae the mixture
– greedy fuckin cake.

There's a knock at the door. Fuck. Ah ignore it. Ma heid is
beginning tae throb again and ah decide it's time tae hit the
bevvies. Ah've enough cans of special tae see me through till
the cookin's over, if nae fucker comes in. The knocking starts
again, only this time it's louder.

–Stevie, ah know yer in there, open the fucking door.

It's Spanner, ma so-called best mate. No way am ah
sharing any of this gear wi him, but he's gaunnae take the
door off the hinges. Ah open up.

– Moan in Span, it's guid tae see yer. Can you spot me a
twenty til ma giro arrives in the mornin.

It nearly fucking works. He's aboot tae turn round, but
his nose must still contain some traces of functionality,
because he starts sniffin the air like a dug.

– Yer cookin up, Stevie. Ah kin tell.

He goes straight in tae the kitchen and by the time ah've
closed the door he's opened one of ma cans and is holding
his heid over the pan, breathing deeply. What kin ye do?

There's a mountain of the brown stuff in the pan, so ah
grease two cake tins and pour the mixture in. Ah can hardly
wait. Ah'm tempted to eat it as it is, but the last thing ah
need is a fuckin bad chocolate trip. The tins go intae the oven
at 200 degrees. Ah cook everything at the same temperature;

ah fuckin hate those yuppie bastards with their fan-assisted bollocks and temperatures. When you're cookin, you're cookin, end ay fuckin story.

    –How long Stevie?

Spanner's as desperate as ah am.

    –Aboot an hour.

    –Kin it be quicker?

    –Ah'm cookin as fast as ah can and yer nae fuckin help.

Spanner's aboot as much use in the kitchen as an amputated prick at a hoor's convention, an ah can tell he's been oan the bevvies. While he's away for a pish, ah put the dark chocolate in a pan and measure oot the caster sugar. Ah add the cream and Kahlúa tae the pan. Kahlua's a fuckin lassie's drink, ah know, but it's no bad in a cake. When ah go tae the scales for the sugar Spanner's already there, aboot tae start shovelling the white powder up his hooter. I dinnae shout stop, but the penny soon drops. He's greetin like hell as he sticks his nose under the tap, while ah'm stirring the sugar into the pan.

    Ah kin hear someone calling ma name. For a moment ah think it's a voice in ma heid, calling me back to planet earth, but ah soon catch on. It's another fucking unwelcome visitor. They'll go soon enough; but Spanner, ever useless, opens the windae and shouts down. Hiddy and Gav are standing in the street, suited and booted. They both work for Grenson's the undertakers, and the two cunts have come around in the company car. Ah owe Gav a fifty and he's no one tae forget. What does he expect? Gav and Hiddy are the only poor fuckers tae get a job, since the social caught em signing on fer five different addresses. They'll no be riding the giro d'écosse for a while.

–Stevie's cooking up.

Ah'm tempted tae lift Span's feet and tip him oot the windae, the big-mouthed cunt, but ah dinnae have the strength. Gav and Hiddy are soon at the door with what sounds like a battering ram. Spanner lets them in, while ah grab another can of heavy before those greedy bastards drink the lot. Gav staggers in looking the man, in a black suit and tie.

–How long Stevie? We've got tae nash.

Hiddy is behind him and between them they're carrying a fuckin coffin.

–Sorry Stevie, the last time we left the car it wis stolen. We got the car back but the body wis missing. It's the sack if we lose another.

Hiddy kin barely breathe. The effort of climbing the stairs has nearly finished him off. They dump the box on the floor and Hiddy collapses into a chair, the skin on his face stretched like cling film over his skull. He could swap places with the man in the box and you'd no notice the difference.

Ah go to close the door and see a wee lassie standing in the hall. She's wearing a black coat five sizes too big and her face is as white as a sheet. Ah look at Gav.

 —Aw Stevie, this is Debbie. That's her boyfriend in the box. We'll no be long, Debbie, moan in.

 She has the look of one of those lassies whae'll do anything tae please. She isn't makin any fuss aboot her boyfriend's little detour on his way to his last resting place, that's fer sure. She sits oan the settee hugging hersel. She's nae bad, she won't be oan her puff for long. Ah'll fuckin move in there, pretty sharpish an aw. Then ah notice she's nae hugging hersel; she's holding a bairn under that big coat. It starts greetin and she gets oot one of her tits tae feed it. The cheeky slut's only breast-feeding, in ma hoose. Ah what the fuck, ah've got tae finish the icing. Gav and Hiddy hae forgotten their hurry and are hittin the bevvies, their feet up on Debbie's boyfriend's wooden overcoat. If it fits him like Debbie's coat fits her, the poor bastard must've been a midget.

 The hour is nearly up. Ah warm through the icing and remove the cake tins from the cooker. Ah find a syringe and needle, ideal for checking the middle of the cake is cooked. Nae problem, the needle is clean. Oan the outside the cake is burnt, so ah cut off the burnt bits and slap on the icing while it's still hot. The two slabs sit there glistening, like bars of brown bullion. Spanner has by now drunk the rest of the

Kahlúa, and is oot of his box, jumping around desperate for a piece of the brown stuff. He can fuckin wait. Ah'm feeling sorry for the wee lassie so she'll come first – after me, of course. The crowd are all smiles as ah come into the room wi a big plate of chocolate salvation, and Debbie's boyfriend makes a nice wee coffee table.

We're all soon stuffing our faces, though ah would'nae recommend the heavy as the ideal accompaniment. Wee Debbie is getting in the swing. She's put the bairn oan the floor wi a piece of cake to stop his greeting and she's cramming a piece of the dark slice intae her gob, her eyes rolling back in her head, like if she eats enough chocolate it'll stop all the pain. Spanner, as usual, has overdone it. The Kahlúa does nae mix well with the heavy, the cake and whativir he had before he arrived. He's back at the windae; who the fuck is arriving now? But he's no talking; he's spewing intae the street, lazy fuck. Spanner is the original come-back kid, and two minutes later he picks up the last piece of cake.

–It's no bad – he says – But it's no the same as skag.

No bad? The fucker's eaten huf of it.

Gav and Hiddy are back on their feet, struggling tae pick up their quiet friend.

–Thanks Stevie, we've got tae nash, says Gav – Don't forget that fifty you owe us.

Ah'm just in time to remove a plate from the coffee table before it's repossessed, and they're away. But ah've goat Debbie's address. Ah look oot the windae: down below they make a pretty wee procession, all in black, weaving from side to side, like Archie Gemmill in slow motion. But the car's no looking too good. Spanner's scored a direct hit. It looks like some fucker's tried tae give the car a chocolate icing, but Gav and Hiddy dinnae notice and they're soon loaded up and off. What kin ye do? He's no the first person tae be carried in and oot of ma place. Nor is he the first to drive off covered with vomit. But credit tae him, he's brought something new tae the game, the poor bastard. Don't get me wrong, ah dinnae feel sorry for him, ah'll be following in his footsteps soon enough. Ah'm the one ah feel sorry fer. What am ah doing that's so fuckin new? We think we're the centre of the universe, but we're not. What's the universe anyway? It's just a great big fuckin roundaboot that we're all going round endlessly and there's nothing we kin do aboot it. We live we die. End of fuckin story.

Tiramisu

à la Marcel Proust

12–15 Savoiardi sponge fingers
4 eggs
100g caster sugar
Amaretto di Saronno
500g mascarpone
2 cups cold coffee
Cocoa powder

Although the fashionableness of any café and its degree of comfort usually stand in inverse relation to each other, on a cold day in March I found myself on the Boulevard Beaumarchais, in a café, whose owners, from their headquarters no doubt far from the district in which I now sat, had succeeded in finding the precise median such that the establishment offered neither style nor comfort; its combination of brown sofas, blonde wood and red walls looked like it had been delivered in a single packing case, from a world which knew nothing of the one to which it was expediting its wares, the result being a mediocrity so well researched that it shouted its presence. Looking now at the cappuccino served to me in the crude white mug, the surface of which had been whipped into a frenzy of froth and too liberally sprinkled with chocolate, I lamented the fact that my age now required me to stop and rest when my body demanded it and not when my eyes were attracted by something or someone too tempting to resist. Yet when I sipped at the beverage, suddenly the memory appeared; the chocolate powder sprinkled on my cappuccino became the cocoa on the surface of the tiramisu that I had first tasted one evening in the garden at Combray, where my father was holding a small party to welcome the former ambassador to Rome, who had recently returned to the neighbourhood with his daughter.

From this ancient past – its great houses gone and its inhabitants dwindling, like the last creatures of a mythical forest – came something infinitely more frail and yet more alive, insubstantial yet persistent; the memories of smell and taste, so faithful, resisted the destruction and rebuilt for a moment the palace wherein dwelt the remembrance of that evening and of that tiramisu.

The combination of cream and coffee seemed to offer access to a world more real than that in which I sat, this pretender that announced itself the 'home of coffee', whose distinct signage of 'Simply Delicious', 'Come in for Lunch', 'Hot Panini' called to a generation to whom I was lost. Did any of its clientele know of the beauty of the Café Florian on St Mark's Square where my ancestors had once taken coffee with Byron? The memory gone, I sipped again at the hot beverage; once more the recollection came of that first

experience, the evening at Combray when I was introduced to Ursula Patrignani, her body flexing like a prima ballerina, bowing in a show of mock courtesy as she handed me a small bowl of tiramisu, and of the slight dizziness I felt in her presence as I looked at the movement of her exquisite Botticelli mouth, too dazed to hear her words. The very unsteadiness of my legs became the rocking of a gondola, as we docked at a Venetian Palazzo and walked arm in arm through the mist into a room graced by Bellini's *Feast of the Gods*. Again the memory faded, and the decaying eau-de-nil walls of the palazzo and the works of the Venetian masters were replaced by red and brown panels and over-enlarged photographs depicting young people in casual dress drinking coffee. I feared that the recipe was lost to me forever.

The creamy draught had cooled; its flavour seemed to be dying already and with it remembrance of that evening. Sensing that the memories had not departed forever and were lingering like souls after death, I ordered a second cup of the milky drink which might in other circumstances have disgusted me; now I craved it as if it were the elixir of youth and capable of curing my old age. "The same, Monsieur?" asked the young waitress. "I am sorry but before I gave you one flavoured with almond syrup by mistake." The poor girl looked anxious, but I nearly kissed those delicate white hands of hers from gratitude; it was the sweet almond taste that had awoken that beauty from its sleep in the dark forest of past memory, recalling the Amaretto di Saronno that I had tasted for the first time that night with Ursula Patrignani in the gaslight among the chrysanthemums. The waitress smiled as she served what was for her just another drink, but for me the liquid was a hallucinatory potion that could open the doors of my perception; her consciousness had barely registered my presence because I was only partly in her world, choosing to probe this portal to truths which dwelt in a realm more real than hers.

This time I closed my eyes and sipped deeply of the draught, realising that what I sought dwelt not in the cappuccino but within myself. This white-hooded potion was my guide down to the underworld, and would assist in shaking free the anchor that kept these elusive memories so firmly held in the depths of my consciousness.

Separate from the others we now talked; hidden by the chrysanthemums, and knowing that no one could see how foolish I must look, I gathered my courage, resolving to ask her to marry me there and then, but as I opened my mouth to speak she gently fed to me a teaspoonful of the delightful mixture, and I was silenced. Never before had I accepted to take food in such a way except from my mother as she gave me my medicine before kissing me goodnight. As I swallowed the heavenly concoction I found myself imbued with an unknown courage; I had to make her understand what I was feeling. "I am experiencing something that I have never felt before," I told her, but before I could continue, she spoke. "I know, it happens to everyone the first time. Chef's tiramisu is simply sublime; Father says that it has saved us from a thousand international incidents and that without it he could never have maintained a peaceful Europe. Madame Verdurin has tried everything to get the recipe, but Father wouldn't give it even to the Duke of Milan." My feelings for her were so intense that I grew light-headed, confused my thoughts with my speech and became unsure of what I had said out loud or thought to myself. Did she feel anything for me? Could she find it in her heart to reciprocate the profound feelings that I had for her? Involuntarily I cried out, "I must know." Whether she really misunderstood me or coquettishly chose to interpret my question in such a way as to keep alive the tantalising doubt that made my mind so feverish, she continued, "You shall know. Chef begins always with the coffee, fresh and strong, but chilled in ice, so that it doesn't dissolve the Savoiardi, the little sponge fingers that are sent regularly from Italy. These he dips into the coffee, turning them, before laying them in the bowl to form the foundation for his creation. The secret is that he always laces the coffee with the amaretto, which he keeps at hand throughout the process." I could barely remain on my feet.

"He then takes the eggs and separates out the yolks, which he mixes with sugar to form a soft cream. The whites he whisks into a snowy peak." To throw myself from that snow-swept mountain. "He then reunites the two mixtures," o blessed union, "before adding the mascarpone a little at a time and a final splash of the amaretto. He then spreads the creamy concoction on top of the sponge fingers and continues with alternating layers until the last layer of cream, which he covers with cocoa powder shaken from the sieve, taking care not to miss an inch." At this I staggered backwards and fainted.

When I recovered consciousness I was in my bed at Combray, my mother touching my shoulder to wake me. At the touch of her hand I looked up. "I'm sorry, Monsieur, but would you mind moving to a smaller table?" A group of young mothers with perambulators waited in the doorway, looking towards me. My cup sat empty on the table and I walked out onto the busy Parisian boulevard.

Coq au Vin

à la Gabriel Garcia Marquez

	Marinade:
1 whole chicken, c. 3 ½ kg	2 medium onions
800g baby onions	1 sprig of rosemary
200g smoked pork	1 small bunch of thyme
2 carrots	3 cloves
5 cloves of garlic	Coriander and mustard seeds
3 sticks of celery	Juniper berries
3 leeks	Red peppercorns
A few leaves of sage	1 litre red wine
Olive oil	

Father Antonio del Sacramento del Altar Castañeda sat in the garden and watched the afternoon die. The darkness had begun to grow as heavy as the heat, and he held off going into the inferno of the house as long as he could. But he had smoked his last cigar and was now unarmed as the mosquitoes enveloped him, and he was forced to retreat into the gaslit interior.

The light of the kitchen dazzled him as he closed the door on the swarm. He slapped his neck, killing a winged intruder before it could feast, and reflected on the last rites. Earlier that day he had visited the murderer Fidel Agosto Santiago to hear his confession, but the prisoner had declared himself unready. Santiago would eat his last supper the following night, and since the condemned man refused to accept food

from his wife, the priest had taken on the responsibility. He sprayed the room with insecticide and began to cough.

Guiltily he looked across at Tobaga, the haughty mulatta who had prepared his evening meal every night for the last fifteen years. Watching her in the kitchen was a pleasure he had denied himself in his more venereal years, but that appetite was now a faint glow whose embers' warmth would only be extinguished by any attempt to refuel them. As she washed her hands he felt the need to urinate and left the room. His once powerful flow, which had reverberated in the night bucket with the sound of a stallion galloping, was reduced to a trickle, the intense ammonia smell of which rivalled the fumes that drifted in at dusk from the swamp and filled him with the sadness of decay.

When he returned to the kitchen Tobaga was preparing the marinade that would bathe the cockerel, that toughest of birds, for two days. "It is for Fidel. The Syrian's servant came today with the cockerel." The priest sat down and thought of the task that awaited him at the prison, but was startled from his thoughts by the sound of Tobaga chopping the bird into pieces. Each time she brought the cleaver down her dress swayed and the contours of her body made themselves more visible. She dropped the head into a bucket and Father Antonio felt a sharp prick on his neck, before bringing his hand down and killing the last survivor of the earlier siege.

Tobaga sliced two onions and added them to the cockerel in the pot. She covered the pieces with wine and, as they bathed in the blood-red liquid, she added juniper berries, coriander, mustard and red peppercorns, cloves and, finally, the rosemary and thyme. She then left the pot to marinate in the marble-lined pantry, the only cool place in the house, and one to which Father Antonio would retreat on afternoons of calamitous heat.

"When will the food be ready?" he asked.

"The marinade must be allowed to work for forty-eight hours," answered Tobaga.

"Can it be shorter?"

She looked at him, her eyes like golden almonds. "For a bird such as this?" And he knew it could not. The cockerel was a gift from the Syrian. Known as El Jaguarcito, The Little Jaguar, it had been the most successful of all his fighting birds. It had earned the Syrian a small fortune and its sacrifice was a mark of the debt he felt towards the condemned man. The priest turned a blind eye to the gambling and bloodshed of the cockfights but knew enough of El Jaguarcito's reputation to understand. "I will speak to the mayor in the morning."

Father Antonio rose, as he always did, at five, and dressed in darkness. Outside dawn struggled to rouse itself as he walked the short distance to the church. The carnivorous cloud had descended once again and he raised the hood of his cassock until he was safely within the nave. As the worshippers arrived, each brought with them their own grief, an emptiness that dwarfed the nave. The insomniac was already there; it was rumoured that he had not slept for 75 years, except during Mass. The second to arrive was a woman who had recently lost her second son; like the first, he had been bitten by a rabid dog, but before the disease had been able to reach its violent zenith she had poisoned him. The last to arrive was the wife of the condemned man. The priest spoke without conviction and the Mass was brief. When the chance to leave came, pausing to remove a cockroach from the font, he headed in the direction of the mayor's house.

Like a marionette, whose strings might break at any moment, the town was stirring. A pair of black macaws flew overhead and the priest quickened his pace. A boy emerged from a temporary shelter at the side of the river and howled at the moon; he laughed at his joke and the priest shivered. Further on he overtook a family that appeared to be pushing all its belongings in a cart. A little girl led the way marching solemnly as she carried a vase of black peonies, and a boy at the rear of the family group held a cage which contained a white dove.

The mayor was half-dressed and sat with his braces over his bare shoulders. His wife did not greet the priest but silently poured coffee for the two men, looking on with her black-ringed eyes. "Thank God," said the mayor. "Another two hours before we start sweating again."

"I need a stay of execution," the priest said, without looking up from his coffee.

"Impossible. The soldiers are already on their way. They will arrive tomorrow."

"He has requested coq au vin and it will take two days to prepare."

"So it's true that the Syrian slaughtered El Jaguarcito?"

"El Jaguarcito is sitting in a pot in my kitchen."

The mayor crossed himself. "Can it not be cooked today?"

"Tobaga says it will be a crime before heaven. We cannot give Fidel Agosto Santiago a half-cooked last supper."

The mayor had no wish to disappoint Father Antonio or the condemned man, who had at one time been the greatest chef in the area. He sipped at his coffee and walked out onto the balcony. "If I agree, it will be to honour the Little Jaguar, not from sympathy for Fidel Santiago." Father Antonio knew that he had succeeded.

"Will you be at Mass on Sunday?" the priest asked as he was leaving.

"Say a prayer for me, Father."

A troupial was singing as the priest headed for the prison. Fidel Santiago sat gambling with his guards. One of the soldiers had lost his horse to the prisoner. The prison house was full of tobacco smoke and the priest coughed. When Father Antonio gave Fidel the news, the condemned man let out a deep sigh. "Tell her not to forget the sage, Father, just a few leaves."

The men returned to their gambling and the priest went out into the growing heat.

On the eve of the execution Father Antonio took up his position at the kitchen table and laid out the church accounts. Tobaga crossed herself, took the pieces of the Little Jaguar from the marinade and allowed them to drain. In a pan she heated the olive oil and added the small onions, whole. She chopped the smoked pork into small pieces and put that, too, into the pan. Into this last arena, slowly and with great circumspection, she now laid the pieces of the Little Jaguar. The body parts spat furiously as they touched the burning oil. When the flesh had turned golden Tobaga covered the carnage with the blood-red marinade and El Jaguarcito was silenced forever. She cut the carrots finely, her breasts making a little jump each time the blade struck the chopping board. The garlic cloves she left en chemise, their paper-dry covers like the sleeping pupae of butterflies that will never emerge. These she threw into the mixture, before adding the celery, leeks and seasoning. She covered the pan; the flames probed inquisitively at its base as she left it on a medium heat for an hour or so. His accounts untouched, Father Antonio closed his eyes and slipped into a siesta while Tobaga kept the vigil, never allowing the pan to run dry, constantly adding liquid from the marinade.

When the time came, Tobaga lifted the pieces of El Jaguarcito from the sauce. As she did so Father Antonio woke with a start. "Sleep on. I will wake you when it's ready," said Tobaga.

"I was dreaming that the food was poisoned and that the firing squad, refusing to be cheated, took me in his place."

"They may yet come for you."

Tobaga passed the sauce through a sieve, then, after touching the liquid and sucking on her finger, added more salt and continued to heat it. When she found the consistency she was seeking she returned the pieces of the cockerel to the liquid and added the sage leaves. A quarter of an hour later she woke the priest with a look. "The cockerel is ready," she said, and she saw the fear in his movements as he rose. "I can take the food to him, if you wish," she added.

"You can go later, but I will hear his confession first. He will not eat until his conscience is clear." And Father Antonio took up the dish and went out into the heat of the evening. As Tobaga watched him go she saw the carnivorous cloud descend to accompany him; the mosquitoes would feed as far as the prison.

Mushroom Risotto
à la John Steinbeck

Extra virgin olive oil
25g porcini mushrooms
3 field mushrooms
1 onion
2 cloves garlic
200g risotto rice
500ml vegetable stock
Salt and pepper
60g Parmesan
1 glass white wine

The porcini lay dry and wrinkled, each slice twisted by thirst and the colour of parched earth. When the water finally fell, at first only in splashes, they drank what they could, but soon they were all covered with the life-giving liquid. The parched fragments recovered an earlier form, their contortions changed, by the gift of water, into a supine mass, glistening. What had resembled a bowl of tree bark now had the rich colour of cooked meat, the purple brown of wet soil had replaced the dry plaster of Arizona earth. The cook left them like this to soak for 45 minutes.

The first oil, extra virgin, poured into the heavy-bottomed pan, and as the flame licked at the metal, it grew more liquid. The field mushrooms were cool to the touch. Their thin skin

and soft white bodies yielded to the knife and the slices piled up on the chopping board. The cook wrinkled her nose as she caught the scent of hot oil and lowered the heat before frying the mushrooms. Their pale flesh soaked up the green liquid, and as the heat surged up through the pan, they turned brown and golden, their once perfect matt surface now shining with an oily sheen.

The heat was now everywhere and irresistible. The fire flared up, steady and unbroken; without a flicker the flame worked at the underside of the pan. The cook wiped her brow with her hand as she turned the mushrooms, browning in the pan. Once ready they were put to one side. Fresh oil was added. The porcini were poured into a sieve; their liquid, dark and brackish, she collected to be used later. Nothing was wasted. The drained porcini slid sizzling into the hot oil, which struggled with the water in their flesh. With a cover the cook muffled the voice of the porcini. The steam condensed on the underside of the lid and dripped back into the pan, recreating the cycle of the rains.

Her scarred and calloused hands peeled the onion and garlic before chopping them finely. She knew the porcini would make it if the pan didn't dry out; the moisture would be needed for the work ahead. When ready, the porcini, too, were set aside and the onion and garlic took their place. Their scent rose like a cloud and the cook stood back, her eyes smarting. The onion grew transparent and soft and gave of its juices. She covered the vegetables with a lid. They murmured and whimpered until they turned to a soft juicy pap. Then the rice rained down onto the onion and garlic, each drop glistening as it was turned in the oil. A drought rain taking moisture where it fell, the rice began to soak up the liquid. As it was added, the porcini stock made a rushing, bubbling sound, like waves breaking at Pebble Beach, and the white grains began to swell, slowly. Soon the liquid was gone. Seasoning was added, and now the vegetable stock was needed, a little at a time, like the movement of the seasons.

The Parmesan cheese was hard and dry. The cook grated what little she had. The cheese grated coarsely, like maize from the thresher; the cheese grated finely, like the first powder snow; the cheese grated in shavings, like the wood thrown up from her husband's plane. She divided the Parmesan and mixed half into the nearly cooked rice, along with the mushrooms and porcini. The mixture grew thick, and she poured on a shot of white wine before giving a final stir.

She shared the mixture out carefully in the cracked bowls, and sprinkled on the last of the Parmesan. It wasn't meat and potatoes, but at least her family would eat tonight.

Boned stuffed poussins

à la Marquis de Sade

2 poussins
85g butter
1 large onion
110g button mushrooms, sliced
55g fresh white breadcrumbs
2 tablespoons fresh parsley, finely chopped
Grated rind of a quarter of a lemon
30g prunes, soaked overnight
30g dried apricots, soaked overnight
Salt and freshly ground black pepper
Half a beaten egg
170g mixed chopped onion, carrot, turnip and celery
290ml chicken stock
1 bay leaf
Watercress to garnish

Should not the supreme aim of gastronomy be to untangle
the confusion of ideas that confront mankind, and to provide
this unfortunate biped with some guidance as to how he
should conduct himself and his appetites? Buffeted
continually by the studies of scientists, the inventions of
dieticians, the fashions of restaurateurs and the disguised
marketing campaigns of a thousand trade associations, his
own tastes are often his last point of reference. The tyranny

C. 05

of political correctness, undermining him further, makes of him a man who avoids endangered species, factory farming, deforestation, genetic modification and inhumane slaughter. If he is unfortunate enough also to have a religion, then he will probably live the meanest of lives in the most tightly fitting of gastronomic straitjackets. By walking such a culinary tightrope, he believes that he will reap his rewards in long life, good health, moral superiority and in heaven hereafter. Yet all around him our unfortunate sees good vegetarians pushing up daisies, teetotallers' hearts tightening and sugarphobes queueing in dentists' waiting rooms. Reader, recognise that all your years of abstinence and your naive trust in low-fat yoghurt have not saved you from a pot belly, heavy jowls and an inadequate sex drive. A life of dieting has rendered your face pinched and furrowed from harsh judgement of your fellow diners and your evenings long and lonely.

Not all of our revered chefs eat the food that they recommend so strongly to us and there are many whose appetites are best expressed behind closed doors. It is with these observations in mind that we take up our pen, and in consideration of their wisdom we ask of you, reader, your full attention for this recipe which I recommend to you, told to me by an innocent girl, Justine, who recently had the good fortune to come under my tutelage.

Judge Hugon was one of these high priests of abstinence, and his table was noted for its correctness. Dressed only in black and white, his visits to the local church struck fear into the preacher, who felt the eye of the judge upon him as if the Almighty himself were standing in judgement. The judge was noted for his rectitude in all matters and his home, frequented by lawyers and politicians, was a fortress of political correction. The judge had taken a vow of abstinence from all unworthy food: endangered cod, non-line-caught tuna, prawns farmed amid the destruction of mangrove swamps and the meat of all living creatures possessed of a soul. Finally, the further to set him apart from his fellow men, his wife, once in possession of three fine children, had invited him to sleep in the guest room.

One afternoon a knock at the door disturbed the judge from his correspondence. He found on the doorstep a timid-looking girl, her delicate countenance a picture of modesty. Her virginal air and large blue eyes, clear complexion, bright white teeth and beautiful blonde hair demonstrated a candour and good faith that were sure to lead her into trouble. This charming young girl was, in fact, the daughter of the local butcher and, when her father's deliveryman had been taken ill at work, in good faith she had offered her services. Unfamiliar with the poor script of her father's employee, she had misread an address and now found herself, not at number 27 The Avenue, home of a well-known bon viveur, but instead delivering two fine poussins to number 21, residence of a man who had renounced all pleasures involving flesh. This is her tale as she told it to me:

"The house was grand and at the end of a long drive bordered on both sides by a high hedge. The black door looked so grand, in fact, that I was quite in awe and, knowing that I was very late with the deliveries, due to my misfortune in the residents' parking area, I was little prepared for the stern figure who opened the door to me. 'Oh sir, I am sorry to be so late with your poussins. My van was clamped and I have had to finish the last of the deliveries on foot.' I must have looked exhausted from my exertions and my voice seemed to touch a chord in the judge. 'Sweet child, I forgive you,' he said breathlessly. 'Won't you come in and drink something?' Looking left and right, he took the package from me and showed me into a long hall. It was not cold in the house but I noticed that he was trembling as he closed the door. 'I'm sure we can deal with the clamp on your van.' The judge made me answer a number of questions, while he listened with an air of great piety. 1. Was his house definitely the last delivery of the day? 2. Was it true that I was not expected back promptly at my father's shop? 3. Was I sure that once the deliveries were over I was to take the day off? 4. Had I parked the van well away from the house?

"When I had fully satisfied him on these points he seemed to relax. 'There, there, my child, so you won't be missed for a while, and we have plenty of time to deal with these birds, I mean, deal with your stranded vehicle. Let me make a quick telephone call; my office has few benefits, but I am, I hope, not without some power in dealing with your current predicament.'

"He was a very large man, closely shaved with pale skin and piercing grey eyes, and for some reason I was beginning to regret accepting his help. 'I have troubled you enough already, sir; I will walk back to the shop and tell my father.' This seemed to make him angry: 'Are you afraid of a member of Her Majesty's bench? Do you doubt that I would act in any way but that which is most just? How dare you.' With that, he grasped my wrist and shoved me into what appeared to be the pantry. I heard the door being locked from outside and found myself alone in the dark. I banged on the door shouting for help but when there was no response I gave up my cries. As my eyes adjusted to the darkness I could see I was in a small storeroom, lined with shelves on which stood well-ordered packages of wholewheat pasta, boxes of GMO-free oats, packets of rice crackers and jars of sugar-free jam. Noticing the keyhole, I bent down to look through. The sight that met my eyes left me trembling. 'O holy father, am I to be the victim of my good nature and daughterly devotion?'

Boned stuffed poussins

"Outside, the judge was slowly peeling away the wrapping to reveal two fleshy white birds, breasts uppermost. I saw his eyes widen and he began talking to the two poussins. 'What have we here? Two naughty little birds.' As he spoke he gave one of them a playful slap. 'We will need to teach you a lesson.' Placing a hand on each bird he gave them a squeeze. 'You have nothing to fear, my little chicks; it is I who am corrupted. Whilst I will break my vow before heaven and must expect the harshest judgement, your innocent souls perch in paradise.'

"He then began to bone the poussins with a kitchen knife. I'm sure my father must have done this on many occasions but I had never watched before. The judge was labouring over the task and sweat dripped from his forehead onto the plump white birds. The job took him some time and he strained and grunted as he worked, using such language that you will forgive me if I refrain from reporting every word of his frightful discourse. Reaching a pause he looked up from his work towards the pantry from which I witnessed his abuses while trembling for my own safety, and he appeared to address the poussins: 'Now, my chicks, you have been well and truly boned. But there is so much more that we can do; how about a little stuffing?' And he took a packet of butter and placed a lump into a pan to melt over a low heat while the villain chopped a large onion. He proceeded to cook the onion gently and then added some sliced button mushrooms. As I watched him, now chopping a bunch of parsley, the odour of the food began to drift in through the keyhole and as my appetite reminded me that I had not eaten since breakfast, I momentarily forgot my predicament.

"I was soon reminded of my situation when my captor began muttering to himself. Although I could not hear him clearly I caught the words 'fresh, white, succulent fruit', and nearly fainted with fear when I saw him walking towards my prison door. I covered my eyes and instinctively cowered on the floor. The door opened and I felt his footsteps as he entered the pantry. Then I heard the clink of glass, and the door slammed shut again as he left. Had my sobs roused some mercy in this monster? I looked through the keyhole, expecting to see him doubting his vile course of action, but was instead greeted by the sight of him arranging three jars on the worktop: prunes, dried apricots and breadcrumbs. He added the breadcrumbs and a good handful of the chopped parsley to the onion mixture, before grating some lemon rind on top and stirring in the chopped dried fruits. He added salt and pepper and, finally, the beaten egg.

"All the time the judge's eyes seemed crazed by a deep hunger that had cast aside his judgement leaving only a determination to satisfy his bodily appetites without check or hindrance; I trembled as I witnessed this eruption. The white shirt that had seemed so well laundered was now splattered with blood and butter stains. I watched, horrified, as he licked the beaten egg from his fingers and then wiped them down his shirt. If he had answered the door in such a state he could never have taken advantage of my naivety. He now laid the two poussins down in front of him and began to stuff them with the mixture. I had no idea that a small bird could take so much stuffing, but he carried on, using language that my ears could barely suffer, until the poor birds could take no more. Then he took a needle and thread, sewed up their openings and patted the brutalised creatures back into shape. He dropped another knob of butter into a large flameproof dish, and as it foamed with the heat, browned the poussins lightly all over. Meanwhile, the villain had chopped some winter vegetables – onion, turnip, carrot and celery – and these he exchanged in the pan for the now golden poussins, and added a little more butter. I could not see clearly but believe that once the vegetables were lightly browned he placed the poussins back into the pan and added some chicken stock. I was horrified to see him do this using a stock cube; if the old scoundrel had not been in such a hurry he could have made a bouillon using the chicken bones. He added a bay leaf and seasoning and then covered the pan and allowed it to simmer for three quarters of an hour. I must have fainted, for, when I next opened my eyes, the cooked poussins were being placed in the oven to keep warm, and Judge Hugon was passing the vegetables through a sieve to extract their juice. He discarded what was left of the crushed vegetables and continued boiling the liquid. I gathered from his study of the spoon that he was waiting for it to take on a honey consistency.

"I feared that once this miserable creature had satisfied the most pressing of his desires it would not be long before this excess of debauchery would overflow and I should become the dish that would feed his baser appetites. I saw that a small ventilation panel high in the pantry might be forced open if I could reach it and disguise the noise of my escape. Climbing up the shelves, I began screaming to be let out and throwing boxes of low-sodium salt and soya milk to the ground. As I suspected, my abductor remained engrossed in his stuffed birds and cared not a whit. At the same time I began striking at the ventilation panel using a tin of vegetarian pâté. At last the mesh gave way; as the light flooded in I could see below me on the pantry floor a pool of white liquid made up of soya milk and rice drinks running under the door. Wasting no time I squeezed my shoulders through the gap and wriggled my legs through behind me. I found myself in the space between two houses. From fear and relief, I could barely stand; I headed for the neighbour's house, on the door of which a small plaque read 'Sir Michael

Mead, MP'; here, surely, was somebody of authority who could help a poor maiden in distress and would see that the judge got his just desserts. I rang the doorbell and fainted."

You may well imagine the politician's distress on finding this poor creature on his doorstep, her clothes stained and her pulse weak. As Justine recovered her senses on his couch, the member of parliament comforted the unfortunate girl as she watered the fine fabric of his soft furnishings with her tears, until they had run their course and she was able to recount the unspeakable happenings of that day. As she spoke, the kindly man took pains to remove all trace of her suffering: the most delicate morsels were served to restore her strength, and while her clothes were taken to be washed, he arranged for the release of her father's delivery vehicle. By the time that Justine left the residence of the honourable member, assured that the accusations against Judge Hugon would be more successfully pursued by a man of influence such as himself, she felt sure in the knowledge that she had found a protector, a man of power with a good heart and respect for those weaker than himself.

No scandal followed, nor was the judge's reputation damaged in any way. Shortly after these events he was appointed Master of the Rolls, and his neighbour, the honourable member, was made a government minister. The two men were both influential at a local level and offered their support to a successful supermarket chain seeking to open a large branch in the elegant neighbourhood. Within a short time Justine's father's shop had failed, and with it his health. His devoted daughter was obliged to take on evening work in a fried chicken take-away establishment. And so it was that I had the good fortune to discover her there, late one night.

You, who have shed a tear for the misfortune of one so virtuous, you, who pity the unfortunate Justine, take comfort. If, through forces that it is not given us to understand, God allows her to be persecuted on earth, it is in order to compensate her all the more in heaven hereafter.

Clafoutis Grandmère

à la Virginia Woolf

500g cherries
3 eggs
150g flour
150g sugar
10g yeast, prepared in warm water if necessary
100g butter
1 cup of milk

She placed the cherries in a buttered dish and looked out
of the window. The children were racing across the lawn,
Nicholas already between the clumps of red-hot pokers,
turning to wait for the others. Looking back at the cherries,
that would not be pitted, red polka dots on white, so bright
and jolly, their little core of hardness invisible, in pity she
thought of Mrs Sorley, that poor woman with no husband
and so many mouths to feed, Mrs Sorley who knew the hard
core but not the softness; and she placed the dish of cherries
to one side.

Gently she melted the butter, transparent and smooth,
oleaginous and clear, clarified and golden, and mixed it with
the sugar in a large bowl. Should she have made something
traditionally English? (Involuntarily, piles of cake rose before
her eyes.) Of course the recipe was French, from her
grandmother. English cooking was an abomination: it was

boiling cabbages in water until they were liquid; it was roasting meat until it was shrivelled; it was cutting out the flavours with a blunt knife.

She added an egg, pausing to look up at the jacmanna, its colour so vivid against the whitewashed wall. Would it not be wonderful if Nicholas became a great artist, all life stretching before him, a blank canvas, bright coloured shapes gradually becoming clearer? There would be lovers, triumphs, the colours darkening, work, loneliness, struggle. She wished he could stay as he was now, they were so happy; the sky was so clear, they would never be as happy again. With great serenity she added an egg, for was she not descended from that very noble, French house whose female progeny brought their arts and energy, their sense of colour and shape, wit and poise to the sluggish English? She added an egg, whose yellow sphere, falling into the domed bowl, broke and poured, like Vesuvius erupting into the mixture, like the sun setting into a butter sea. Its broken shell left two uneven domes on the counter, and all the poverty and all the suffering of Mrs Sorley had turned to that, she thought.

When the flour came it was a delight, a touch left on her cheek as she brushed aside a wisp of hair, as if her beauty bored her and she wanted to be like other people, insignificant, sitting in a widow's house with her pen and paper, writing notes, understanding the poverty, revealing the social problem (she folded the flour into the mixture). She was so commanding (not tyrannical, not domineering; she should not have minded what people said), she was like an arrow set on a target. She would have liked to build a hospital, but how? For now, this clafoutis for Mrs Sorley and her children (she added the yeast, prepared in warm water). The yeast would cause the mixture to rise up into the air like a column of energy, nurtured by the heat of the oven, until the arid kitchen knife of the male, cutting mercilessly, plunged itself into the dome, leaving it flat and exhausted.

Little by little she added the milk, stopping only when the mixture was fluid and even, smooth and homogenous, lumpless and liquid, pausing to recall her notes on the iniquity of the English dairy system. She looked up: what demon possessed him, her youngest, playing on the lawn, demons and angels? Why should it change, why could they not stay as they were, never ageing? (She poured the mixture over the cherries in the dish.) The dome was now become a circle, the cherries surrounded by the yeasty mixture that would cradle and cushion them, the yeasty mixture that surrounded them all, the house, the lawn, the asphodels, that devil Nicholas running past the window, and she put it in a hot oven. In thirty minutes it would be ready.

Fenkata

à la Homer

1 rabbit
2 onions
3 cloves of garlic
Extra virgin olive oil
10 fresh plum tomatoes, peeled
1 tablespoon tomato puree
Rabbit herbs (2 sprigs each of thyme and rosemary, and
*   a handful of flat-leaf parsley, all roughly chopped)*
75ml red wine
2 medium potatoes, peeled and chopped into small pieces
2 carrots, peeled and chopped
A handful of peas, preferably petit pois
2 bay leaves
Seasoning

Sing now, goddess, of the hunger of Peleus' son, Achilles.
Tell me now, you Muses of Olympia, daughters of Zeus, of
the empty-bellied Achaians, whose supplies were grown old
and stagnant while they stormed the great walls of Ilion for
ten long years. You who know all things, while we have heard
only the rumour of it and know nothing, tell me now of the
cunning of resourceful Odysseus who, when he saw the
hunger that spread through the strong-greaved Achaians, as
obliterating fire lights up a vast forest along the crest of a

mountain, was not dismayed, but stood forward to take up his bow and his cauldron of bronze.

Now, when rosy-fingered dawn showed, Odysseus stirred from where he was sleeping and slung his bow over his shoulder. He bound the fair sandals beneath his shining feet and went on his way into the sand dunes. Soon he came upon a swift-footed coney grazing in the dunes, and now Odysseus the godlike, holding his bow and his quiver full of arrows, bent the bow before him and let the arrow fly. Nor was his aim untrue, but Apollo, who strikes from afar, was still angry with the strong-greaved Achaians and sent the arrow astray so that it fell harmlessly in the sand. Now the startled rabbit began to run to take cover, swiftly as a mountain stream, which gains speed before disappearing beneath the glistening rock, only to appear later in some unexpected place. But Athene appeared to Odysseus and told him to shoot a second arrow, though it seemed hopeless; and this time he did not waste his strength; the bronze-weighted arrow found its mark and passed through the liver and came out the other side and undid the strength of the rabbit's legs, and its black blood drenched the sand and its eyes were shrouded in darkness.

Odysseus bound the mighty creature's feet and slung him over his shoulder to carry back to the Achaians' camp on the beach of the grey sea, beneath the bows of the wooden ships.

Then swift-footed brilliant Achilles gave up his weeping and came out from his tent. He girt about his chest and loins a leather apron and skinned the rabbit and cut it expertly into equal parts. Then he took the pieces and fried them in olive oil until they were brown and the smoke rose up to high Olympus, where sit the gods who rule over men. Seeing Achilles the godlike no longer brooding in his tent, Menelaos took courage and came with herbs and seasoning, which he added to the cauldron. Then resourceful Odysseus mixed the sweet wine in the bowl and poured it over the meat and removed the cauldron from the fire, to allow it to marinate for thirty minutes.

Atreus' son, wide-ruling Agamemnon the powerful, chopped the onions and shed tears, as a stream dark, running down the face of a cliff impassable, sheds its dim water; but raging that it was not king-like, he would chop no more. Now Achilles chopped the garlic and, in a separate cauldron given by Agamemnon, fried the onions and garlic, nor did he stop frying until the onions began to brown. Then he added the tomatoes, the puree, the vegetables and the bay leaves to heat and simmer for fifteen minutes. Now Nestor the wise, with the guidance of Athene, persuaded them to combine the contents of the two cauldrons into one. This they left to simmer over a cool part of the fire for one hour, so that the rabbit was soft and tender. Then Achilles offered up a prayer to mighty Zeus of the wide brows, and he poured the wine into the mixing bowl and looked up into the sky. "High Zeus in far Olympus, hear me as you have heard me before and did me honour and brought to pass the wish that I prayed for. For see how I myself have worked hard with my hands and cooked the rabbit and made offerings of the vitals. Grant that the food is good and that my work is appreciated by the Achaians, and not only when my hands rage invincible against the Trojans, and that the meal will be eaten in good spirit without dispute among the lords of the glancing-eyed Achaians." So he spoke in prayer, and Zeus of the wise counsel heard the son of Peleus and granted him one prayer but not the other. That the food should be good he allowed, but refused to let the meal pass in harmony.

But resourceful Odysseus was mindful of the appetites of the Achaians, and when the dish was ready he took the sauce to serve on platters over linguini as a starter. Now Agamemnon stood forward and claimed the biggest portion, "Since I am king and greater than all here so that no man may contend with me." He spoke thus and then sat down, and the anger came on war-like Achilles, so that his heart was divided two ways, whether to take up his sword and kill Agamemnon or whether to put aside his anger and serve him the worst portion. Then in answer spoke Achilles unto Agamemnon, lord of men. "You wine sack with a dog's appetite, my portion you threaten to reduce for which I laboured much. When the Achaians cook, do I have a share that is equal to yours? Though always the greater part of the cooking is the work of my hands, when the time comes to dispense the rations, yours is the far greater reward."

Now Nestor the horseman stood forth among them and spoke to them saying, "Proud Achilles, beyond others you are strong in battle, not one of all the Achaians will belittle your words nor speak against them, yet you have not completed your arguments. But let me speak, since I am older, and go through the whole matter, since there is none who can dishonour the thing I say. I will speak in the way it seems best to my mind, and no one shall have in his mind any thought that is better than this one that I have in my mind, either now or long before now. Let lots be shaken for all of you to see who wins which portion." So he spoke and each of them marked one lot as his own. They threw them in the helmet of Atreus' son Agamemnon. And Achilles set before each of them a portion, according to their lot. Nor was any man's hunger denied, and they put their hands forward to the good things that lay before them and ate until they had put away the desire for eating and drinking.

Vietnamese Chicken
à la Graham Greene

¹/₂ teaspoon grated lemon zest
3 cloves garlic
2 tablespoons fish sauce
1 tablespoon soy sauce
1 teaspoon finely ground black pepper
¹/8 teaspoon cayenne
2 boneless chicken breasts
2 tablespoons dry sherry
2 tablespoons lemon juice
2 tablespoons peanut oil
1 teaspoon molasses

A recipe has no beginning or end: arbitrarily one chooses
at what point the cooking instructions become necessary,
after the butcher has done his work and before care of the
dish passes to the seasoning whims of the guests. I choose
the moment when, looking into the refrigerator, I noticed the
naked white flesh of the chicken. As I stared at the breasts
I felt a pain across my head. The sound of church bells
announced evensong from across the darkening Common,
and I sipped at a gin and tonic. The tonic was old and had
lost its sparkle, leaving a bitter taste, but it was now too late
to get anything fresher. The rain drove against the window,
and water was collecting on the sill where it refused to close.

I acknowlege my transgressions: and my sins
before me.

Vietnamese Chicken

The smell of chopped garlic clung to my hands as I mixed it together with the lemon zest, fish and soy sauces, and the peppers, black and cayenne. The chicken breasts rested on the counter and my hand moved towards them as though guided by an unseen force. It was too late to go back; she would be here soon.

Ritually I sliced the breasts into thin strips. The white flesh lay on the plate like a shredded contract and I hurriedly threw it into the marinade. The soy and fish sauce splashed across the meat, like ink smudged in the wet. I covered the mixture and returned it to the refrigerator. Two more hours would be ideal, but if the chicken soaked for half an hour it would be all right. I thought that in future I must do better.

While the flesh marinated in the cold darkness I mixed together the sherry, molasses and lemon juice. I poured another gin, without tonic this time, and turned on the wireless. The choral music was interrupted by a reading, Psalm 51. I turned off the set, but I knew the reading and it continued silently in my head as I heated the oil in the wok until it was smoking.

I took the marinated breasts from the refrigerator and tipped them into the burning oil, turning them with a fork. When the chicken was almost ready I added the sherry sauce; the rich liquid thickening made a sharp contrast to the whiteness of the steamed rice I would serve with it. I had failed to wear an apron, and as I stirred more rapidly, the rich concoction splashed onto my white shirt. I wiped at it with a cloth but the stain grew worse. In my frustration I called out "Damned ...", but before I could finish I was interrupted by a knock at the door.

Sole à la Dieppoise

à la Jorge Luis Borges

2 fillets of sole
¹/₂ litre mussels
100g button mushrooms
50g butter
125ml white wine
Half a lemon
1 tablespoon plain flour
Salt and pepper

The story that I shall tell concerns an incident that took place in London early in 1944. Its protagonist was proclaimed a hero by both sides of the conflict, yet its consequences favoured only one, and led to the downfall of a seemingly invincible tyrant with an insatiable appetite.

Early in the Second World War, fearing invasion, the British removed all signposts from their highways. The intention was that spies and invaders would find themselves lost in the endless labyrinth of Celtic curves that make up much of the British road network. The task of overseeing the project fell to Sir Henry Smith. Inspired by the British initiative, a Parisian restaurateur, Amadée Antonin, removed the place names from all dishes on the menu of his small hostelry. For a short while, German officers dining in Antonin's restaurant found themselves lost in a recondite

menu without signposts. The entries for such dishes as Crayfish à la Bordelaise and Lobster à la Parisienne offered the diner no guidance as to the possible fates of the unfortunate decapods, and Paris Brest could only be ordered by those who had known the menu since childhood.

It was in the old Confitería Águila that I first came across Sir Henry Smith's story. A small item in the Buenos Aires journal *Carne y Producción* noted the anniversary of his death and gave brief details of his career. Later, during a lecture tour of Germany, I stumbled upon another report of Sir Henry Smith or of a second Sir Henry Smith. Here the story grew deeper and more complicated. The article concerned papers from the wartime government, only recently released, in which reference was made to Sir Henry as 'The Spying Knight of the Reich', German intelligence's highest-placed agent during the Second World War.

My lecture tour moved on to England and there I spent much of my free time researching the strange history of Sir Henry. From privileged access to the journal of his last days, written in the cuneiform he had learnt as Woolley's amanuensis at Sumerian Ur, I have tried to create a full picture of his final hours, faithful to the facts where they were available. As may be expected I will alter one or two details. Here is his story.

It was on 2 March 1944, at 1 p.m. precisely, that Sir Henry Smith turned into Great College Street and, before the chime of Big Ben had faded on the air, remembered the note that he had been handed as he left the House of Commons. Sir Henry read the single line that occupied the page. Fearing that he might faint, he steadied himself against a wall and refused an offer of help from a passer-by. The note was from his contact, Agent 42, who had recently been directing Sir Henry to pay particular attention to information that might indicate the location of a probable Allied invasion of France.

The imminent capture of Agent 42 inferred Sir Henry's own arrest and execution. In the few minutes required to walk home, and from the infinite choices that lay before him, Sir Henry decided upon his plan of action. From the small bookshelf in the kitchen he took down a little-thumbed volume and his glacial eyes began to scan the index: Cod à l'Anglaise, Cod Provençal, Crayfish à la Bordelaise, Fish Soup à la Nimoise, Sole à la Dieppoise. Satisfied, Sir Henry scribbled a note that he passed to the concierge with a large tip and instructions that the fish was not to be filleted.

Sir Henry, feeling the relief of a murderer who finds himself under arrest, sat on the sofa by the bookcase. He opened a volume at random and began to read. The pages told the story of Astyages, whose merciless numina had brought to him the rule of Persia, and who defined his invincible purpose through the dream interpretations of the Magi. On their advice Astyages ordered the death of his own grandchild. When his orders were frustrated by the disobedience of his general, Harpagus, Astyages butchered the latter's son and served him cooked to the nescient father. At the end of the meal the boy's head and hands were brought to the table. Harpagus made no show of revolt, but in secret sent a message, hidden in the stomach of a cooked hare, to Astyages' (now fully grown) grandson, Cyrus, promising the general's collusion in any attempt to overthrow the tyrant. Fearing discovery, Harpagus sent a second message, concealed in the boiled carcass of a turtle, urging all speed, which arrived before the first and gave rise to the apocryphal tale of the Greek fabulist.

The book grew heavy and Sir Henry fell into a sleep. He was visited by the same dream that had recurred at intervals over the preceding months. He found himself in a vast maze, whose creator was observing from a tower as the dreamer ran through the green corridors of the rain-drenched labyrinth, trying, unsuccessfully, to take an unseen direction or to make an unpredicted move. Sir Henry was awoken by the return of the concierge, whose trip had been a success. He left the minister with a pint of mussels and a single sole, with the spine still attached.

Sir Henry was neither an accomplished cook nor a habitual piscivore, but he prided himself that, as a loyal servant, he knew how to follow instructions. Opening the recipe book, he cleaned the mussels and left them to stand in a bowl of fresh water while he made a telephone call to a journalist on *The Times*. Reports tell us that the journalist agreed to come to Sir Henry's apartment at 8 o'clock that evening, on the understanding that the minister had a story for him. Sir Henry then seasoned the sole with salt and pepper and placed the pieces in a flameproof pan. The sun had by now descended below the rooftops and through the window he perceived the tower of Westminster Abbey. The light of the gas flame took over from the extravagant sunset and illuminated Sir Henry's irremeable countenance. He drained the mussels and recovered them with the fresh water so alien to their nature, discarding as irretrievable any that did not close when tapped. He fried the mushrooms in a little butter and squeezed some lemon juice over them, covering the pan to preserve the juices. Meanwhile, he redrained the shellfish and placed the covered pan over a gentle heat, shaking it gently until all the bivalves were open, again removing any that did not conform with the majority. Sir Henry drained the liquid into a bowl and removed the mussels from their shells. The mushrooms were now ready and he poured the liquid from their pan over the sole, then added a glass of white wine and the juice from the mussels, so that there was just enough liquid to cover the fish.

Among the unread books in Sir Henry's library sat

Augustine of Trieste's treatise on asceticism. Confronted with
a meal of fish, Augustine postulates the argument against
carnivorism. Once eaten, the fish would transubstantiate into
the flesh of the anathematised eater, and, for Augustine, to
whom this fish was Sir Henry's own ancestor, its
consumption was no less than cannibalism. He brought the
liquid to simmering point and poached the sole with
measured chronometry. On the stroke of the eighth minute
Sir Henry lifted the sole from the liquid and placed it onto a
warmed serving dish. He surrounded the fish with the
mussels and fried mushrooms and kept it warm while he
reduced the poaching liquid by allowing it to boil for three
minutes and 30 seconds. Meanwhile, Sir Henry facilitated
the collaboration of the remaining butter and flour, which he
interpolated gradually into the liquid, stirring continually
until the sauce thickened. He thought of the infinite
possibilities of these few ingredients and of the practicability
of cookery being classified as a branch of mathematics,
rejecting this hypothesis in favour of gastronomy as
language. He poured the sauce over the fish and placed the
dish under a hot grill for a few moments to brown, before
serving it with mashed potato.

Debate concerning the actual ingredients employed is of a
dialectical nature. The recipe book used by Sir Henry
disappeared following the inquest but is likely to have been

the spuriously modernised 1921 edition of *Baron Brisse's 366 Menus*. From the depositions of the concierge and of the journalist, I can hope to have reconstructed the recipe with a fair degree of accuracy.

Sir Henry poured a glass of white wine to accompany his meal, took the front door off the latch and sat down at the table. As the firmament grew dark and the Abbey disintegrated into the gloom, he conjectured that he would not have the honour of facing the opprobrium of his countrymen. The chimes of Big Ben could be heard as the clock struck the hour, and recalling other ancient evenings, Sir Henry offered up a short prayer before beginning his lustral supper.

He was found later that evening by the visiting journalist, his lean, athletic figure sprawled across the carpet, arms outstretched. On the table were the remains of a meal half-eaten and an open recipe book. The following day the late edition of *The Times* ran the headline MINISTER FOUND DEAD. Along with the title of the dish that he had been eating, the journalist had interpolated the detail that Sir Henry's throat had been lacerated by fish bones as he choked to death. Five days later a German infantry regiment was moved from the Normandy coast to a defensive position in the environs of Dieppe, and the first glowing obituaries had already appeared in honour of Sir Henry Smith.

Cheese on Toast

à la Harold Pinter

1 loaf of ciabatta
1 aubergine
Extra virgin olive oil
Pesto
200g mozzarella
2 teaspoons fresh oregano, chopped

ACT I

A kitchen, cluttered. A fluorescent tube is flickering, trying to light. Beneath a window is a sink, piled with dirty dishes. The bin is overflowing with rubbish; nearby, empty bottles are standing. There is a small kitchen table; newspapers and unopened letters obscure the surface. At the table are two chairs. There is the sound of a key in a door, muffled voices. The door bangs shut; instantly HURLEY, a young man dressed in a leather jacket, and CLACK, an older man, tramp-like in appearance, enter stage left.

HURLEY. Come in, make yourself at home.
    (CLACK *enters and looks around*)
    Bloody light. I've been meaning to get a new tube.
    (HURLEY *reaches up and taps the light with his finger until it stops flickering.*) I'll make you something to eat.
CLACK. I haven't eaten all day. I can't remember the last

82

time I had a proper meal. I mean a proper sit-down meal, something hot.

HURLEY. (*Looking in the fridge*) Do you want to use the phone? Call your daughter?

CLACK. What, at this time? I'll call her tomorrow. She won't want to come up here tonight, she starts early in the morning.

HURLEY. I can't offer you much. I haven't done a proper shop for ages. How about cheese on toast?

CLACK. What sort of cheese?

HURLEY. Mozzarella.

CLACK. Mozza what?

HURLEY. Mozzarella. It's Italian.

CLACK. Not for me. I'll have a slice of toast though.

Pause

HURLEY. I must wash this grill sometime.

(*He is holding a grill pan covered with dried cooked cheese. He cuts a ciabatta in half, lengthways. Similarly, he finely slices an aubergine and puts the pieces into a frying pan where some oil is heating.*)

CLACK. Not a bad little place you got here. All yours is it?

Pause

This must be worth a few bob. How long you been here?

HURLEY. I don't know ... about three years.

CLACK. Made a few bob on it, have you?

(HURLEY *puts the ciabatta under the grill to warm*)

That's a big slice of toast.

HURLEY. It's ciabatta.

CLACK. Cia what?

HURLEY. Ciabatta. It's Italian bread.

CLACK. You Italian are you?

HURLEY. Everybody eats it these days: ciabatta, focaccia, schiacciata, panini.

CLACK. Can't you just put me a couple of slices in the toaster?

HURLEY. Toaster's broken.

Pause

I'd like to have a little Italian eatery one day. Nothing fancy, mind. Simple snacks: panini on ciabatta, focaccia, bruschetta; pasta lunches, spaghetti, penne, rigatoni; the basic sauces, pesto, Bolognese, arrabiata. Classic mains: carpaccio of tuna drizzled with truffle oil, pan-fried fillet of beef on a bed of wilted spinach in its own jus. You want a cup of tea with it?

CLACK. Now you're talking. A nice cup of tea.

HURLEY. You ever been to Italy? I knew a bloke there once, bit like you. That was years ago. He's probably dead by now.

(*He removes the aubergine from the pan, the flesh has soaked up the oil and is a golden colour with dark stripes left by the ridges of the frying pan. The ciabatta has now warmed and he spreads a thin layer of pesto onto the cut side*). Where's your daughter live then?

CLACK. My what?

HURLEY. Your daughter. The one who was meant to pick you up at the station.

CLACK. Oh, her.

> *Pause*

> She lives in Catford.

HURLEY. Catford? I used to go to the dogs there. I remember one night I was doing well, nearly all winners I'd picked, till I put the lot on the last race. I did a forecast, two and four. I don't know why, I nearly always did two and four about. But that night I didn't. Only came in four and two. I lost the lot. You a gambler?

CLACK. What, and throw my money away like that? Not me.

> (*Pause as he looks down at his lap*)

> You haven't got a safety pin have you?

> (HURLEY *lays the slices of aubergine on top of the ciabatta and pesto and begins to slice the mozzarella.*)

HURLEY. You can give her a call in the morning. I'll make you a bed up.

CLACK. She works in the morning. I told you.

HURLEY. You like olive oil?

> (*He lays the mozzarella over the aubergine, drizzles olive oil*

on top, and finally adds a sprinkle of chopped oregano,
before placing the ciabatta under a hot grill.)

CLACK. I don't want none of that foreign muck.

HURLEY. Olive oil? It's good for you.

CLACK. It's for cleaning your ears out, ain't it?

HURLEY. (*Drops a tea bag into the overflowing bin*) Here you
    are, a cup of tea for you.

CLACK. (*Gives a sigh of contentment*) You can't beat a nice cup
    of tea.

   (*He sips at the tea and pulls a face*)

   You got any sugar?

HURLEY. Over there, on the table. I don't use it much.

   (*The sugar has hardened. CLACK chips at it with a*
   teaspoon until he has sweetened his tea enough. He checks it
   occasionally throughout the process. The sound of sizzling
   comes from the grill. HURLEY waits until the mozzarella
   has turned brown and golden in places.)

HURLEY. Here you are. It's ready.

   (HURLEY *cuts the two lengths of ciabatta into pieces.*)

   You'll try some, won't you?

CLACK. Not for me. That's no good to a man like me.

   (HURLEY *puts the plate of ciabatta onto the table.*)

   Don't look bad though, I'll give that to you. It's . . .

   Pause

   Well presented. That's what it is, well presented.

HURLEY. I would have done a salad garnish, or a few fresh
    basil leaves if I'd had them.
CLACK. Don't look bad at all.

> *Pause*

> I'll just have a taste.

> (*He takes a piece and bites into it. The mozzarella sticks to
> his beard in long threads. His face brightens in surprise.*)

CLACK. That ain't bad, that ain't. I reckon you might make
    a go of that caff yet.

He reaches for a second piece. HURLEY *is already eating.*
The two men sit in silence, occasionally sipping at their tea.
The fluorescent tube begins to flicker again, but this time
HURLEY *ignores it. Lights slowly fade.*

Curtain

Onion Tart

à la Geoffrey Chaucer

225g plain shortcrust pastry
1 tablespoon fresh thyme, chopped
25g butter
2 tablespoons olive oil
8 onions, finely sliced
salt and black pepper
2 teaspoons caster sugar
1/4 teaspoon each of grated nutmeg and ground ginger
2 eggs, plus 2 egg yolks
425ml double cream
Large pinch of saffron strands

Then spake oure Host.
"Now have we heard from every which one
Of our fellowship with receipts to tell, but one.
Maister Graham, as knoweth many a man,
Loves best tales of cuckoldry as he kan.
And thou, wyfe of Bloomesbury, long of face,
Right boldly hast thou taken thy place.
God knowes well thy stream of consciousnesse,
For your clafoutis may God you blesse.
And thou, clerke of Prague, put away thy bookes,
Tis no time for Ovid, our tales are for cookes.
Culinary are our metamorphoses,
From ingredients chaos, creators we.

Onion Tart

And when such tellers as these turn their voices cleere,
To Ars Culinaria, as they have here,
Nourished are our Christian men's soules,
But no less our bellies, our board and bowls.
And thou, sire at excise, who hath herkened these tales,
All the while taking note and drinking ale,
Telle us some merry dish, by your fay,
For 'tis high time thou entreth in the play."
"Gladly", quod he,
"Certe I can roaste and seethe and broille and frye,
But, as it thinketh me, nought can best a pie.
Therefore I will go tell, as well as ever I kan,
A receipt that will nourishe us, every man.
Now herkneth what I saye.

Here beginneth the Man at Excise's receipt:
On a floured board roll pastry that it be thinne,
Caste thereto with thyme and line a deep tinne.
Trimme the edges neat with a cooke's knyfe,
Then bake it blinde at gasse mark fyve.
Melt the butter and oyle in an heavie panne,
Covered wiv a lidde, as knoweth every man.
Then adde onyons in slices fine ywrought,
And caste thereto sugar and salte.
Cover the panne and turn the heat down low,

Onion Tart

Stirre every while, else the onyons stick to.
Remove the lidde and seethe for ten minutes mo,
That the sauce reducteth and darke growe.
Strewe thereto nutmeg grated, tho keep some by,
And grounde gyngere, and return to the fyre.
Lightly beat the eggs and zolkes together,
And season wiv both salt and black pepper.
Heat the crème till just warme with saffron rich,
Then adde the beaten eggs for to mix.
Spoon the onyon sauce into the pastry case,
Then pour egg and crème custard into the base.
Bake in the oven for minutes xxv,
Til golden brown our tarte be."
"Now", quod our Host, "so God you blesse,
Ye have set an ensample for the rest,
Since ye so much knowen of that art,
And right well have you told us part.
Though in kitchen's cunning there's nought, dear brother,
That in olde tyme was not said by another,
In the way of telling your creation's made,
For none shall remember you by your trade.
Thy customhouse stores much of strange beauty,
And in future with tales will pilgrims pay duty."

Here endeth the receipt of the Exciseman of London.

Rösti

à la Thomas Mann

3 large grated potatoes, parboiled or if large floury sort, grated raw
1 onion, finely chopped
Cheese, Gruyère or Emmental
Salt and pepper to taste
Butter

Von Rohrbach felt himself in a state of strangely reduced vitality and was relieved to be at last gathering his strength in the air-conditioned interior. The morning walk had been overly ambitious and only now that he was at rest was he aware of the blood pounding in his temples and of his shortness of breath. His chest was heavy as he recalled the evil exhalations of the lunchtime traffic and resolved to avoid going abroad at such times as might prove inimical to his health.

The restaurant was well lit, elegant and comfortable. Feeling his fluttering pulse recover, Von Rohrbach ordered a glass of Gruaud Larose and sat back in the comfortable, high-backed chair to look about him. Luncheon was already under way and a queue was now forming at the entrance. Von Rohrbach glanced at the cringing waiter as he placed the glass before him. The waiter was a man of slight build, hardly of the Alsatian type, but tall and bony; the white linen tunic, unbuttoned at the neck, revealed the man's strikingly large Adam's apple and his servile manner made an unpleasant impression on the diner who was presented with a bound volume. A menu it apparently was, but a menu unlike any that Von Rohrbach had ever seen, indeed, compared to it, all other menus with which he was familiar seemed the briefest of notes, the vaguest of sketches; this was a menu devoid of any understanding for the hard-pressed diner, the adventurer wishing to be surprised, this was a menu that resembled the Treaty of Versailles in its scope and in its attempt to exclude all possibility of misunderstanding.

All his life Von Rohrbach had suffered from a sympathetic nerve in his solar plexus. It had afflicted his childhood and now caused him to skim over the pages of beef, pork and game – meats that might heighten his emotional energies or draw blood from the lungs to the heart. The ivory white of the paper calmed him, the rustle of the pages recalled his long hours in the studio. Lingering over the list of exotic dishes – he saw there a trout prepared after the manner of Pondicherry. He had never been to India, the travels of his youth had long since given way to the industry of his later years, the stern service that had brought its share of honours. It was he who had returned painting to its place of pre-eminence among the visual arts, who had renounced modernism and re-ignited the flame of German art. The menu's description wove in his mind a

spell and summoned a picture. He saw, he beheld, a canvas; a group of fishermen returning from the river, around them the forest, thick with mangroves, their exposed roots reaching into the tidal stream, their nets full with an exotic catch, bug-eyed tiger prawns, flying fish brought to earth, spider crabs in their prehistoric armour; the fishermen triumphant, unaware of eyes that watch from the bamboo thicket where the tiger crouches. His brain reeled, his body still wet with sweat, Von Rohrbach sensed the danger, and closed the menu.

The tasteful interior began to fill with guests and the solitary diner released from his exotic study began to enjoy the scene before his eyes. That uniform of civilisation, the business suit, gave outward conformity to the varied types, but most of the principal European tongues could be heard within the confines of the restaurant. A Polish lady and her children were being served at the neighbouring table. They were about to eat when Von Rohrbach noticed with astonishment the perfect beauty of the vegetable accompaniment; that dish most popular in Switzerland but which finds itself reproduced in varying forms elsewhere in Europe: rösti. The rösti, its shape recalling the noblest moment of creation, the grated potato fried to form a cluster of honey-coloured ringlets, the centre thick and proud, golden, its edges burnt darker and tattered like the circumference of the sun, of a chaste perfection of form such that our diner felt his very entrails bewitched. The handsome young boy raised his knife and fork and, as he did so, first noticed the attentions of the older diner. The young lad's strange twilit grey eyes met those of the artist and Von Rohrbach saw, not without excitement, that his attentions were welcomed. As the boy's knife cut into the sweetly yielding centre of the golden disk the artist was utterly enraptured. Shamelessly he followed each mouthful and Von Rohrbach remarked exquisitely that the young lad did not betray him.

The rösti recalled a form and colour from his childhood that he could not place: the golden cluster, exquisitely framed by the viridian Dresden chinaware, the highly polished cutlery, like Narcissus' pool, reflecting the beauty of the dish. Time, which before had crept at a pace barely noticeable, now accelerated and with a stirring of regret Von Rohrbach saw that the beautiful young diner had reached the last few mouthfuls. A feeling of delicacy forced the painter to turn away, unwilling to witness the oily residue that would leave its stain on the surface of the plate.

The master sought the eye of the waiter. Once more time slowed and Von Rohrbach feared lest the kitchen be exhausted of its supply of the tuberous temptation. He sipped of his Gruaud Larose and eventually received the attentions that were his due, from a brutish-looking fellow whose lips curled back into a smile.

"I will have the rösti,"

"Of course, sir, a speciality of the house; may I also recommend the blanquette de veau?"

Suspecting the waiter of trying to increase his tip Von Rohrbach refused, "Just the rösti . . . and another glass of the Gruaud Larose."

He looked once more towards the youth to see if he had noticed the connection that was firmly established between them, but the lad was now in conversation with his sister. Time dragged for the artist, leader of the Romantic Expressionist movement, creator of the heralded work *Victor and Vanquished*, whose every painting was sold before the canvas had dried. There he sat. His eyes, now half-closed, signalling the vanity of the observer who refused to wear spectacles as he watched the doors of the kitchen. Waiters carrying empty dishes disappeared only to reappear, their arms charged anew with offerings from the sanctum, lesser priests who brought news from an unseen oracle to the faithful of the temple, devotees who had been to the very edge of the furnaces from which the sacrificed sent their smoky signals to the gods. A waiter emerged into the light pushing a heated trolley; to Von Rohrbach he appeared no less than Helios the sun god driving his chariot. The restaurant became the firmament and its crossing seemed to last an entire day. The flaming cargo fuelled the fires of the artist's appetite such that all appeared to hinder the passage of the celestial body until it found its resting place in front of the new acolyte, eagerly awaiting his initiation. There before him was laid the Gordian knot, whose solution lay, not in logic, but in the sword and the courage to sweep aside empires. Therein he saw the stellar and the terrestrial, how bewilderingly they mimic each other. The golden buckler lay on the smooth faience, its gilded coils glistening, recalling the reflection on the shield of Perseus.

Dazzled and beguiled, he took his blade and split the disk asunder. At the first mouthful his gaze found the strange twilit eyes of the youth and he was astonished anew – something between a pact and a promise had been established with the young pilgrim who had led him from darkness into light. The sensation was unmistakeable: there was cheese in the galette, surely no product of the valley floor but of higher ground, lofty eyries where hunts the eagle, a Gruyère perhaps or an Emmental. But there came further flavours; the sacred mingled with the profane, a taste from lower ground of onion mixed with the fruit of the new world. As a master mixes his oils in the studio, adding a little more ochre, a touch more vermilion until the balance is right, so Von Rohrbach now sought to penetrate the mysteries that found expression on his other palette. These potato shavings, natural yet incredible and uncanny, had been grated raw and seasoned to taste. Now, inextricably bound with the shredded onion and cheese, they had made the ascension from the subterranean to the extraterrestrial. This holy trinity had faced the fires of the pan together, cooked on a low heat in butter in a lidded pan for fifteen minutes on each side.

Beguiled, Von Rohrbach was reaching the last few morsels; in the final precious moments his eyes rolled upwards moving from side to side as though seeking something that can only be tasted from within. The maître d' had noticed his strange behaviour and instructed a waiter to present the bill; guests had been taken to the sanatorium before but it was not good for the establishment's reputation. Two more members of staff hurried forward and each taking an arm helped the diner from his table. Von Rohrbach's mouth hung open, his lips moved and he rehearsed the possible variations of rosti: "Sauté the onions first, fry with small pieces of bacon, replace the Gruyère with Gorgonzola . . ." Half-carried, half-stumbling, he was led past the table where sat the lovely youth, and his eyes sought again that look of exquisite complicity. But the boy, now laughing as he shared dessert with his sister and mother, was unaware of the painter's departure. As the two members of staff deposited the trembling artist onto the

Moules Marinière

one of that small coterie that reads recipes in bed late at night. Readers of recipes are fickle and a reader such as you certainly has other books on cookery to hand. Without doubt you have already discarded a number of other recipes as unsuitable:

recipes for which you have not the right equipment;
a fish kettle is expensive and difficult to store in your small kitchen;
recipes that are too laborious – the Athens of Aristophanes was run by slaves and the preparation of dormice is long;
recipes too critical in their timing;
recipes unacceptable on religious or moral grounds: pork, dolphin, dog;
recipes that have become redundant. Such is the ease of the ready-made, who now makes jam, bread, pastry (puff pastry least of all)?

But is this the recipe you are seeking? Without doubt you have read the title and are open, at least in principle, to the idea of moules marinière. You have cast an eye over the ingredients and it now seems that if you can find mussels, the preparation will present few difficulties, but your decision will be made at the last minute, according to market price and availability.

You have returned, then. The trip to the fishmonger was a success. At the last moment you were perhaps tempted by the bright eyes of a fish, but you remembered your fear of bones, small, white and sharp, perfectly disguised in the white flesh. Mytilus edulis conveniently wears his skeleton on the outside where we can see it. It comes off in two neat pieces, leaving the little jelly-like body defenceless. But for the moment the black molluscs lie on the draining board and, like armoured troops awaiting their orders, they must be made clean, and presentable. With a knife and under a cold running tap you remove any traces of weed, barnacle or other small crustacea that might be inhabiting the black skeletons of our bivalves.

So now the mussels are clean, each shell black and shining as a hearse. The mourners are crammed into a pan and covered with fresh water. Outside the sound of chopping alarms them – you have begun work on the shallots. Perhaps the guests are here already. Don't allow them to distract you; leave them to drink their aperitifs in another room, or better still ask a guest to chop the parsley while he drinks his glass of chilled Muscadet – that way you can concentrate on other details. What will you serve with the mussels? The oven is hot, but you don't want the guests to see the oven chips poured from the plastic bag; the magic might be broken. Send them away. You knew it was a mistake to let them into the kitchen; the oven is not even hot. If the dish is a starter send one of them to the bakery for a baguette or two.

In a large pan, one for which you have a lid, the chopped shallots are now sizzling in the melted butter with the thyme, perhaps even a bay leaf. You add the garlic, chopped finely. Now inspect the mussels. Reject any that remain open. Like books on a shelf they must all be closed. Like writers, they do not welcome visitors; a tap on the shell and it closes tighter than a priest's breviary. Now cast them into the pan and add the white wine. As the liquid falls onto the hot oil it makes a hissing sound and steam rises. The guests are impressed. You replace the lid and the noise dies down; in five minutes it will be ready. Are the bowls warm? Is the table prepared? Are there candles, wine, wine glasses? The stage must be set. Perhaps you are eating alone. Still there is no harm in making the table a pleasant place to sit. Reading a book is difficult when there are mussels to be eaten; instead you play some quiet music.

The lid of the pan is jumping: the meal is nearly ready, its author almost forgotten. Do you now add the fresh parsley? How much? How soon? You cannot recall and the guests are watching. Having memorised its contents you have hidden the incriminating recipe, and the guests suspect nothing. "A little dish of my own, handed to me by my grandmother ... I improvised." The author is one of many ingredients that can be left out at the time of serving. Confess you have been unfaithful to my text, my own fault, "pepper to taste" showed the weakness which inspired the revolution. There are no shallots? Then onion will do. If we added cream it would be more of a treat, and let's not bother with the thyme. Does a writer of recipes not deserve the same respect as other authors? Do his writings not depend for their creativity on the most subtle of inventions, a well-placed grain of salt, delicate variations of flame and heat? You would not dream of treating writers of "literature" in such a way. *What*? Raskolnikov kills her with an axe? Too violent, a blunt instrument will do: let us say she is knocked unconscious with a rolling pin.

The guests are at the table, there is time to check the recipe once more. You take the book from the shelf one last time for reassurance, only this time the recipe calls for a bouquet garni ... it should have gone into the pan with the onion and shallots. But wait, this is not the same book ... you can hear the guests' voices in the next room, you take down another volume. Moules marinière: yes, there it is, but you now note that the final lines require you to "Add the cream". There was no mention of cream ... you have no cream. Your guests call from the dining room – can they help? "Stay there," you cry. You do not want be seen reading from a book. "It's nearly ready. Choose some music." Where is the original recipe for moules marinière? What is this dish that you have made? What use is a recipe that keeps changing? But wait, this is not the right book. In fury you throw the volume into the empty sink. You would throw it into a pan of boiling water, letting it bubble until it is no more than a thin porridge; or better still you would like to grate it until a pile of shredded paper sits on the work surface. Some words might still be legible and you will settle for nothing less than complete annihilation. You pass them through the mincer, the blender, the liquidiser, so the book becomes so much confetti. You might grind them with pestle and mortar to produce a flour from which you will bake bread and feed it in morsels to migrating birds. Better yet, spread the tiny flakes of print on a pan and scorch them under a hot grill. You envisage the smoke as it begins to rise but the sinuous forms take on the appearance of letters, then words, an affront to your efforts. Let the extractor fan do its work and watch the smoke drawn up, expelled and dispersed into the atmosphere as the tiniest particles, rising beyond the city to be carried off on the four winds. You want to do this, but there is no time, the guests are hungry. Then on another shelf you notice the broken spine. In your haste you have placed the original recipe book not on the shelf reserved for cookery books, but on that allocated to literature. You take one last look, you have only to add the parsley, fresh, flat-leafed, roughly chopped. Cream is optional. You return the book to the same place on the shelf, next to the works of Italo Calvino, and serve.

Plum Pudding

à la Charles Dickens

4oz suet, finely chopped
4oz raisins
4oz currants
4oz plain flour
Pinch of salt
1 rounded teaspoon baking powder
4oz breadcrumbs
4oz moist sugar
1/4 teaspoon ground mace
1/4 teaspoon grated nutmeg
1 egg
1 gill milk (approx.)

The Judge's Chamber – A Christmas Tale

THE FIRST TRIAL

The Artful Dodger was dead, of that there could be no doubt.
His brief light had shone brightly on Jacob's Island and in
the unlit streets of Bermondsey and Rotherhithe, where
many had made him their model. And oh, he had made
them laugh when he stood in the dock, for Fagin had said he
would never peach, not the Dodger, even if he were for the
drop, and he never did. But Fagin was dead, stretched a week

before, so it was the transports for the Dodger. His passage, HMS *Penitent* had gone down in rough seas. Captain and crew had abandoned ship, but the cargo had not been saved, and the cargo was prisoners, flesh and blood, men and boys, chained and shackled, and the great weight of iron had dragged them down and the Artful Dodger had sunk where there were no snuff boxes, nor candlesticks, nor silverware, nor bright kerchiefs, and the Dodger's nimble hands lay among the coral where denizens of other depths picked at him, until he had no more to give. The Artful Dodger was dead, and the newspaper, that Christmas Eve, was as good as a death certificate in the cosy chambers wherein his honour, Justice Hungby, warmed himself by the fire, with his coffee and his toasted muffin, in anticipation of the last case of that year 1842. One of that bad lot, a boy, was to stand that morning before the judge's bench, charged with the violent robbery of items necessary for the concoction of a plum pudding and without doubt, a worthy subject for transportation in the impartial eyes of Tobias Hungby.

"Dism, there seems abroad a morbid and sickly sentimentality about young criminals accompanied by a want of feeling towards the victims of their sins. I trust you do not share it?" The comment was addressed to his clerk, a pathetic fellow who was engaged in removing the carcass of a fly from the windowsill. The clerk, holding the fly by those appendages so essential to the transport from which it derives its name, shook his head while Judge Hungby took a bite of his muffin and a mouthful of coffee. He had booked a good many passages on the *Penitent* and shown as little interest in the welfare of those he sent on their way as he showed now that their voyage had come to its brutal end.

The judge was undistracted from his reading by the chimes of the clock, which was decorated in holly and ivy in token of the season, until, at the eighth bell, the sound turned wet and he saw a drip land with a small splash, and a large measure of impudence, on the green leather inlay of his desktop. Looking up in the spirit of inquiry for which the legal profession is so well known, he saw that a stain had appeared on the ceiling, dark brown in colour and seeming to grow larger by the second. The clerk was summoned, blamed and sent to investigate. The judge read on, taking in several pages of the utmost depravity: an unidentified body washed up by the Thames at Wapping, escaped convicts prowling the Woolwich marshes, a prostitute bludgeoned to death in her lodgings. By way of variety the paper reported the story of a suicide who had drowned himself by tying a bucket to his head before diving into a canal, and it entered the judge's mind to consider what sentence he would have given the scoundrel had the attempt failed. Prison was so often a poor deterrent; it was well known that prisoners were better fed than the law-abiding poor. The judge took another bite from his muffin and pondered the solutions to the tide of crime that threatened to engulf the city – a course of meditation that on this occasion was brought to a halt when a drip struck him squarely on the forehead. With all the authority of his position he glowered at the leak and struggled to suppress a shiver as he now remarked a striking resemblance of the dark patches on the ceiling to the eyes and mouth of a skull. From the mouth the drips had become a steady stream whilst the drops from the eye sockets might have been mistaken for tears.

The water now began to rise and the judge, making to leave the room, found this to be an action more easily projected than done, for the door was now locked. With a growing sense of dread his fingers rattled the knob, his mouth began shouting for the clerk and his fists attacked the door with a savagery usually reserved for his judgments. The fire that had kept the judge's chambers so warm on this cold December day now hissed and spat, before succumbing to the icy flood. Trapped and with the water still rising Judge Hungby made for higher ground. His feet splashed through the dark water, as he stepped first onto his chair and thence onto the desk where he crouched hugging his knees and awaiting the return of the clerical dipterist. The waters gave no sign of abating and were now nearly at the height of the desktop, about which they seemed to be flowing in a circular motion as though the island sat at the centre of some nefarious whirlpool. Holding his hands over his face the judge called again for the clerk, but could not keep his eyes from the dark surface of the water, or his imagination from the flotsam that bumped about the wooden island. The island's inhabitant now grew silent, his eye drawn by anything that moved on the current, his ear by flotsam unseen in the gloom as it bumped against the furnishings and panelling of the chamber. With absorbed attention he now eyed some peculiar item of debris whose identity defied him. The realisation that it was a half-submerged clump of grey hair caused the blood to drain from the judge's face and, were he given to fancy, might have made his stomach to turn a somersault, but he was not. The superior power of his forensic mind prevailed and Hungby stretched out an arm to retrieve his old barrister's wig, but before he could touch the reverend horsehair his arm froze, his eyes widened, and the scant strands rose, as best they could, on his head.

There in the water floated a body, face down, its grey flesh and bloated proportions testifying that it had long been submerged.

In that agony of fear he could not take his eyes from the corpse, carried as it was on the dark flood. The sound of dripping echoed in that little chamber like the ticking of a clock and in the darkness the corpse seemed to glow like a bad oyster. Its black hair swayed like seaweed on the water's surface as the current brought the floating form closer to the desk where, to the judge's horror, its head came to rest with a heavy bump inches from the saucer-like eyes of our terrified castaway.

Like little bells the chains that hung from the ankles and wrists of the body tinkled in the water and revealed the status of the bearer. A large drip fell from the ceiling, and landed with a splash on the corpse's scalp. As though woken from its deathly slumber the corpse raised its watery countenance whence grey eyes met the judge's petrified gaze.

"My snuff's all wet, you wouldn't ave a pinch would yer?"

The judge's blood stood still and a trembling took hold of every limb as the spectre, for how could it be else, came to life.

"Don't you look at me like that, after all it was you what put me in this disgraceful sitivation. Don't I deserve to be lagged on land? Not left to drown in a stinking 'ulk."

The judge was now racked by the most awful chattering of his teeth and seemed to have lost all power of speech.

The phantom continued, "Speak up, man. Guilty or not guilty, 'ow do you plead?"

Seeing the judge's mouth open and close soundlessly the corpse smiled. "Enough of your games, you old scoundrel. Don't you know me?"

Despite its terrible aspect, there was something of the apparition's snub-nosed physiognomy that yet dwelt in the judge's recollection.

"The old Artful Dodger? I was to be the greatest of my time. Didn't the gaffer 'imself say so? Worth fifty times the tuppenny halfpenny snuff box what you lagged me for. Oh, but you could teach the gaffer a thing or two, I'll bet you made a bit of blunt a sending of boys on the transports."

By now the judge was whining and mumbling incoherently.

"Make a note, clerk, the prisoner refuses to reply."

The Dodger was enjoying his part. Now floating on his back he had taken up the judge's wig from the waters to place it dripping above his own flattened brow and taking hold of the lapels of his jacket he was now affecting the learned air of self-satisfaction so familiar in the courts.

"Oh, ladies and gentlemen, we 'ave before us a proper villain. A villain not on the outside, but the worst of all, a villain on the inside with an 'art as black as his gown."

The Dodger looked well pleased with his eloquence and with a great rattling of chains set to swimming backstroke, the irons on his bowed legs chiming like the tolling of a ship's bell.

"Oh, your honour," said the counsel aspirating the h, "These irons is 'eavy. But they were 'eavier still when I was alive and suffering from the fever."

The prosecutor paused at this revelation to see what effect it wrought on the defendant, who had begun to sob out of pity for himself.

"Tears in the court? You won't fool me, you old cur. Call the first witness."

The Dodger's voice reverberated in the chamber as though it were some vast cavern. As the echo died the door of the judge's closet swung open causing a small wave on which the floating counsel bobbed contentedly. Outside snow was falling and a faint glimmer of light reflecting off the surface of the water revealed a man suspended by a noose from the back of the door. The floating prosecutor now addressed himself to the corpse, its mouth agape and its tongue protruding almost onto its chest. "Could my learned friend look around this 'ere room."

It was a habit of Judge Hungby's to find fault with the procedure of counsel and, notwithstanding the dread and trembling that currently occupied his mind and body, he did so now.

"You have not sworn the witness." There was a note of desperation in his usual measured tones.

"Swear 'im? The gaffer? A 'spectable old genleman of his reputation? 'E ain't any cause to lie. Any road I'll 'ave you for contempt."

The witness raised its face, terrible to behold, revealing

the rope which cut deep into the throat and neck; its eyes bulged and a white foam lay upon its lips. It made a rattling sound as though clearing its throat and then spoke.

"Dodger, my dear, you will be the greatest lawyer of the age."

"Thank ee, Fagin. Can you tell the court, in your own words, *Mr* Fagin, the particklers of the crime."

"Yes, my dear, I was minding my own business, a planning of your release, when that villain put this rope about my neck and sent me for the drop. Oh, ladies and gentlemen of the court I did suffer in extremest." The hanged man then pulled a stream of colourful handkerchiefs from his pocket, all tied in a row, and held one end to his eye, whilst being sure to watch the effect they had on the court as he half-sobbed, half-choked

"Try to compose yourself, Mr Fagin, look around this 'ere room and tell the court if you can you see 'im what put that rope around your neck and stretched you so piteously?"

The terrible eyes of the hanged man made a great show of looking in all directions before alighting on the judge, at which the dread countenance broke into a decayed grin.

The phantom raised a bony hand, its fingers protruding from the fingerless glove of faded black and indicated the judge, now coiled so tightly in his robe that he resembled a large beetle with a human head.

"That's 'im," said the pendant witness, "a more bloodthirsty devil, or a tidier murderer I've never seen."

The judge renewed his sobbing, his face had taken on the unwholesome grey phosphorescence of the phantoms that now tormented him and there broke out upon his lips a curious grey foam, like day-old snow, as he whimpered in appeal, "But he deserved to die." Fagin opened his eyes and mouth wide at the Dodger as though his worst crime had been to borrow a cup of sugar and not to return it.

"The witness is not on trial," said the Dodger with a yawn, as if this old ruse were tried every day. "And don't address me, man, address the jury." He began to chuckle, still swimming playfully on his back. A smell of sulphur filled the chamber as the defendant looked around the room for evidence of the committee in question. He heard the voice of the prosecutor, "Gentleman of the jury, 'ave you reached your verdick?"

"Hold your noise." There came a deeper voice from within the chamber and from the shadows stood forth a huge man dressed in the coarse cloth of the prison, the arrows painted on his clothes pointing upwards as if to draw attention to his massive head, in which his one eye, half-closed, seemed to be winking. His nose was almost flat and its irregular contours suggested that it had been incompletely and unskilfully flattened with a blunt instrument, and the figure's horrific aspect was made the more disturbing by the presence on his head of a judge's forensic wig. The man, or spectre, or demon climbed up onto the desk and made the defendant stand. Anyone could see that Judge Hungby shook with fear as he leant on the spectre to support his trembling legs. A noose fell from the darkness above and hung before the judge's face. While the condemned man begged for clemency, and promised an end to transportation, the huge convict tied the judge's arms, fastened the noose about his neck and then stepped down into the water to join company with his fellow phantoms. As though through a picture frame the judge caught a last glimpse of the three officials of the court. Waist deep in water they looked back at him. The Artful Dodger and the Convict removed their wigs to bow, Fagin, meanwhile, with one hand held up the end of the instrument of his own demise and curtsied, in a movement seldom seen but graceful to behold. The three accomplices then placed their hands on the desk, braced their bodies, and, as the dodger called aloud "Heave!", the great mahogany desk began to move. Two more heaves and the judge teetered on its edge, unable to gain any purchase. He struggled for a few moments before his feet gave way and he dropped. The tightening noose cut short his scream and with a terrific convulsion of the limbs Tobias Hungby lost consciousness.

THE SECOND TRIAL

"Sir, the court is waiting." The clerk's hand on Judge Hungby's shoulder woke him, the morning newspaper lay on his lap, the heat of the fire burnt his cheek, the clock on the mantelpiece, dressed still with holly and ivy, chimed the o'clock as the judge put his hand to his throat.

"Dism," he addressed the clerk, "what day is it?"

"Why it's Christmas Eve, sir," the clerk addressed the judge.

"Then there has been no inundation of my chambers?"

"No, sir, the leak was occasioned by the clerks above, sir, upturning a jug of porter in premature high spirits of the season."

"Then I have not been on trial for my life. O glorious day, o wonderful clerk, Dism, o season of joy, quick, quick help me into my gown!" Judge Hungby examined his forensic wig, as though he now held it for the first time, before placing it over no great quantity of hair, and showing an expression of such contentment that I doubt has ever been seen beneath that token of authority in general and I am certain had never been seen beneath that token in particular, he addressed his clerk with, of all things, a smile. "The case, Dism, o wonderful boy, what is this morning's glorious business?"

"A series of robberies, your honour, with violence. A boy, stealing from a grocer's and fruiterers," the clerk replied.

"Poor boy." There was a smash as the clerk dropped the coffee cup that he was removing. "Hunger, Dism, is a terrible thing. Would that Famine might stand one day before me in the dock. Now is the season to chase him from the world." And with that he ran from the chamber, leaving the clerk gathering the pieces of broken crockery.

The courtroom could hardly have been more crowded had Famine indeed been on trial in Judge Hungby's court that Christmas Eve. Outside the sun struggled to make himself known from above the cloud that had settled over Holborn and the city, and could do little to raise the temperature on such a cold December morning. The clean white snow sat high up on the rooftops and dripped down into the dirty snow that lay in the streets and found itself churned and begrimed by the passing traffic. Shoppers performed like circus entertainers as they carried improbable numbers of parcels, and grocers and poulterers watched queues form as they struggled to cope with the demand at this time when all eat more heartily than on any other day of the year. Yet some still found leisure to fill the gallery for a chance to see the guilty pay for their crimes, or to warm their hands and feet before the spectacle of the law. A young boy of eight or nine years of age stood in the dock, his face so wan, so prematurely old, like so many of his kind. Only a wooden crate enabled the little creature to be seen behind the iron spikes that served to keep such ferocious creatures from the good men of the bench.

Mr Bisquiz appeared for the prosecution. He had a small mouth and eyes, and whiskers that struggled to grow in the hard ground of his countenance so that his face seemed decidedly underfurnished. His angular body was similarly sparse and appeared, with all of its sharp angles, to be ideally suited to the prising open of sealed containers. Bisquiz's techniques rarely failed in the court of Judge Hungby and he painted a dark picture of young Tom White, the prisoner. He might appear young in years, Bisquiz argued, but he was old in the crime of the streets, and that the crime for which he appeared in the dock today was unlikely to be his first offence and even less likely to be the most serious of offences that lay behind or before him.

The shopkeeper, Mr Tartberry, was called to the witness box. A well-fed gentleman with red hair, redder cheeks and a black eye took the stand. He was sworn and then stood twisting his hat as though wringing water from wet laundry, till finally overcome by the attention of the court, he stared down at his boots. On being pressed, Mr Tartberry described his long suffering at the hands of the accused and of his fellows, writhing and groaning with each grievance in such a way as gave the court to understand that his losses had been severe and might well have included the theft of some one or more of his vital organs.

"I was serving one of the ladies of the neighbourhood, Mrs Chickenstalker it were, with some of my finest Norfolk Biffins when I saw the boy place a handful of raisins in his one pocket and a handful of currants in the other."

"A great quantity of dried fruit would you say, Mr Tartberry?"

"I should say, about four ounces of each, sir."

"Did you then challenge the thief?"

"I did, sir, though I was struck dumb when I saw him place a quarter pound packet of flour into his trousers. I am not so young as I was, but I excused myself from Mrs Chickenstalker and wasted no time in chasing the prisoner. But boys can be awful quick, sir."

"Did he flee the premises?"

"He did, sir, he fled all around them premises, while I chased him and Mrs Chickenstalker attempted to lay her bag on him. She's a powerfully built woman, sir, and would have killed him outright for sure with one blow of her shopping bag, and spared us all a morning in court."

"No doubt the two of you proved sufficient to see off the juvenile?"

"No, sir, the little wretch was not leaving until he had all he wanted. He ran alright, not out, but round the shop, a holding onto his hat and looking about him until he snatched up a quarter pound of moist sugar from the counter."

"The scene must have been most distressing for you, Mr Tartberry?'

"I'll say, the boy would've murdered me with running after 'im if Mrs Chickenstalker's shopping bag 'adn't laid me out like a like a blow from the blacksmith's 'ammer."

A policeman was then called to describe the circumstances of the arrest. Following Mr Tartberry's complaint and the theft of four ounces of suet and an egg from a nearby butcher's shop, the police had forced an entry into a building in Calthorp Street, whereupon a motley crew of men, women and boys had fled the building by window and rooftop, some few escaping over the wall that stood at the back of the residence. The house was deserted except for the prisoner who was found in the basement tending a pudding.

"And is it true, officer, that you did find the paper I have here in my hand constituting a confession and projecting a more serious attack on Mr Tartberry's premises?" Pressed to reply with a yes or a no the policeman had no alternative but to reply in the affirmative.

"I hold here in my hand a scrap of paper upon which has been written, 'Mace and Nutmeg'. I hesitate to encourage the ladies and gentleman of the court to imagine what violence our young plotter intended for Mr Tartberry and those who would stand in his way. Harmless he may look, but I never saw a juvenile more bound for the gallows. Who here would care to see the prisoner at liberty, armed with mace and ready to nutmeg us in our beds for a pound of raisins?"

The prisoner's large eyes peered over the side of the dock as he struggled to recognise himself in this portrait. He had suffered a good many beatings in his short time but never had he been able to give the same in return, not even with the aid of the aforementioned instruments.

Anticipating the judgment, more people had filled the gallery and newcomers feeling the warmth of the courtroom removed their snow-covered hats and comforters. Habits long held die hard and despite the charitable spirits with which he had opened proceedings, Judge Hungby was growing impatient. His court had seen men condemned to hard labour on less evidence than this. The prosecution's case was made and lunch was beckoning when, from a comforter which had been left to hang from the gallery, some melting snow fell onto the courtroom floor. The splash landed within earshot of the wigged authority and caused that instrument of justice no small consternation. At almost the same moment there came an almighty crash in which Judge Hungby imagined that he heard also the rattling of chains in the hold of a ship and the sound of the tide breaching a bulkhead. Fearing the worst the judge fell to his knees imploring the unseen force to spare him.

"Your honour, the boy seems to have fainted." It was the policeman who spoke to the now cowering judge.

"What?"

"The boy, sir, he's half-starved."

"The boy? Fainted? Wonderful news." An expression of relief suffused the judge's face, as he hurriedly prevailed the policeman to help him up from the floor. "Poor boy, I mean. Officer, take him through to my chamber."

The shopkeeper, blinking, stood now the sole object of the court's attention and tried to affect a relaxed expression.

"Mr Tartberry." The judge addressed the witness.

"Your honour?" The witness addressed the judge.

"You have had ample opportunity now to view the defendant, have you not?"

"Yes, I have, your honour."

"And on this occasion the defendant was stationary, was he not?"

"Begging your pardon, your grace."

"I mean, he did not run away."

"No, sir, not this time, 'e couldn't."

"More time to study him, would you say, than on the occasion of the theft from your premises."

"Oh yes, indeed, sir."

"So it would be fair to say that you now have a very good idea of the appearance of the boy in question."

"Oh yes, your worship, I'd know 'im anywhere."

"Excellent, excellent, Mr Tartberry. Would you then describe him to the court."

The grocer, surprised by the sudden turn of events, showed the expression of a man who has just realised that his purse is missing.

"I will not hurry you," said the judge, hurrying the witness.

"Well, 'e was small, small for his age I would say, with a cunning roguish look in 'is eye."

"I have a pretty large experience of boys and they're a bad set of fellows at that, but that they are small, with a roguish look, would appear to be an aspect common to all boys. Mr Tartberry, for the benefit of the court, could you describe this boy in *particular*."

"Quick 'ands 'e 'ad, and deep pockets and no respec' for 'is elders, like the rest of his gang."

"Thank you, Mr Tartberry, but in what respect did he differ from the rest of his kind?"

The grocer, who could have told a currant from a raisin, an orange pekoe from a ceylon, a wax candle from tallow, seemed unsure of how to tell one boy from another.

"Would you tell us what colour were his eyes, or the colour of his coat?"

Mr Tartberry hesitated.

"I have no wish to hurry you, but the range of colours is not great."

"They were blue, a cold blue." The witness bit down hard on the side of the knuckle of his index finger and thinking better of his words, "A green blue, with touches of hazel. And he wore a green coat."

Judge Hungby's face beamed, surprising all who were familiar with his manner and suggesting that the witness's precision had now secured a rapid conviction and an early lunch.

"Usher, would you bring the defendant back into the court."

There was a general gasp as the boy returned, his head bowed, his too long sleeves covering his hands; he stepped up onto the box to be seen by the court. His brown coat was faded and tattered unlike the rich brown of his eyes that gazed out fearfully on all the majesty of the law.

At this manifestation of the shopkeeper's error, a great roar rose up from the gallery and broke like a wave upon the court and over its foam and surf came the judgement of Hungby: "Case dismissed! Tartberry, bring the pudding."

THE THIRD TRIAL

So clerk and counsel, judge and gaoler, prisoner and policeman gathered in the judge's chamber. Tom took his place at the table where sat the pudding, and Mr Bisquiz inquiring as to its manufacture learned how Tom had sifted the flour, salt and baking powder and had mixed these with breadcrumbs, suet, dried fruit, sugar and spices.

"Does that not make for an awful dry mixture?" inquired the judge.

"No, sir, not once I added the egg and milk and mixed it well. Please, sir, then I turned it into a well-greased basin, which I covered and steamed for five hours."

And old Bisquiz, holding up his portion before the lamp to examine its colour, and poking and prodding its surface to test its texture, finally consented to place a morsel in his too hollow cheek where he could find no false note in the flavour of the pudding. And even Tartberry, who was in no small hurry to return to his busy shop, allowed that if they were his dried fruits then they were put to uncommon good use and that he might shift a good many of the puddings next season if Tom White had a mind to make them with good ingredients, honestly come by. And all agreed that there had never been a better pudding nor a better Christmas Eve. And the ruddy, brown-faced, broad-girthed pudding sat and gleamed to hear itself talked of in such terms, shining in the fatness of its new steamed glory and urging and beseeching one and all to share in its eating. As for Judge Hungby, looking on as his companions laughed and feasted about the same desk upon which, only that morning, he had feared to breathe his last, he could find in his heart no word of criticism for the pudding, that he judged to be a good one. In such company even Dism caught a taste of optimism for the new year, and young Tom, who had never before sat among such genteel folk was so exceedingly grateful for his deliverance from the charges, for the warm fire at his back and for the laughter that shook the judge's desk, but most of all for the rich, sweet comforting taste of the plum pudding, one mouthful of which was as good a safeguard against hunger and low spirits as a man can hope for, that he cried aloud, "God bless us, every one."

THE END